Smiles

+ Duct Tape

Anne -
    thanks for
being part of our
duct tape!
            ♡ Jess Torrey

JackO

Smiles

+ Duct Tape

by

Jesse Torrey

Deeds Publishing | Atlanta

Published by Deeds Publishing in Athens, GA
www.deedspublishing.com

Printed in The United States of America

Cover and text design by Mark Babcock

Library of Congress Cataloging-in-Publications data is available upon request.

ISBN 978-1-944193-69-0

Books are available in quantity for promotional or premium use. For information, email info@deedspublishing.com.

First Edition, 2016

10 9 8 7 6 5 4 3 2 1

To Jack, Anna, Dan and all the smiles and duct tape that have held our family together.

Prologue

I had the "talking" dream again last night. I have one every couple of weeks and I always wake up hopeful. It's so vivid and almost always exactly the same.

I walk into Jack's room to wake him and find him sitting up in his bed. He gives me one of his magical smiles. As I open the blinds, I say, "Good morning, Jack."

He looks at me and says, "Hi." It's clear enough to make me pause, but I don't get too excited—I've been let down before. I lower his bed rail and help him to his feet. As I start to get him dressed, he leans his head against mine and says, "Good morning." I don't just hear the words, I feel them on my face. He doesn't pause. He just keeps talking. Filling me in on the last ten years of his life.

I still can't believe that it's been ten years since I've heard Jack speak. If I'd known that he was going to lose his speech, I would have focused more on his last sentences. I would have treasured them, taped them, hung on every last word.

When Jack first stopped speaking, we thought he was just too uncomfortable. We'd heard that it isn't uncommon for patients to shut down after a stem cell transplant. It's part exhaustion, part mouth sores, along with overwhelming frustration. Besides, we were too focused on blood counts and surviving to notice as the words slipped away.

It wasn't until after Jack's transplant that I stumbled upon an article that discussed issues facing Adrenoleukodystrophy (ALD) boys post-transplant. Loss of speech was on the list. Ten years ago, I didn't know that there was a list of "post-transplant ALD issues." I didn't know what ALD was or that the disease would one day be the center of our family. Ten years ago, it never occurred to me that I would only hear my eighteen-year-old son speak in my dreams.

Before my husband Dan and I had ever heard the word Adrenoleukodystrophy (ALD), we didn't realize how perfect and easy our lives were. Great marriage, two beautiful children, lovely home, one lucrative and one creative career (Dan with the first, me with the second), and an abundance of incredible friends and family. We loved the new phase of having school-aged children, preferring the "learning to read stage" to the "changing diapers stage."

Now we're back to changing diapers and learning to read seems laughable.

Jack was eight years old when he started the second grade in the fall of 2006. He'd always been a delightful and fun-loving kid. He was a decent student, and liked school and playing with his friends. But as that fall progressed, Dan and I noticed that Jack was acting strange. I don't know how else to say it. He wasn't finishing anything (homework or bed-making or teeth-brushing). He always seemed tired and distracted. He started having a difficult time finding the right words and increasingly chose to stay quiet. Once, I found him naked in his room, staring at the wall. "Jack, what are you doing . . . Jack?"

He looked lost before finally hearing me, then seemed startled and covered himself. His explanation was that he had forgotten what he was doing.

Some days I would scream and threaten and other days I would cry in frustration. Dan and I spoke to his teacher, who encouraged us to get some help. Learning specialists and pediatricians led us to an Attention Deficit Hyperactivity Disorder (ADHD) diagnosis. The ADHD diagnosis led us to neurologists and psychologists, then more talk of ADHD, of therapies, of behavioral techniques. We tried everything, but Jack kept slipping. He started chewing everything from his shirts to his socks. He started touching himself inappropriately and lost all boundaries with others. His handwriting became so illegible that schoolwork was impossible. By Christmas of 2006, we knew there was something profoundly wrong with Jack.

More doctors—more tests. Nothing worked. His teacher's comment, "18 years of teaching and I have never seen this kind of regression," landed us in Jack's neurologist's office with me crying and begging for an MRI. We needed to answer one question—What is wrong with Jack?

The tears worked, and two days later we were at our local hospital for an MRI. Within hours, Dan and I were told that Jack's MRI showed serious inflammation in his brain. I remember asking the doctors if it could be cancer or a brain tumor and being relieved when they assured us that it was neither. Little did we know that there are far more evil diseases that can lurk in a child's brain.

After five days of doctors and tests, our local hospital gave up and transferred us to New York-Presbyterian Morgan Stanley Children's Hospital in New York City. The ambulance driver was confused when Jack walked himself onto the ambulance, held up his hand and said, "Hello." How could this child be sick enough to need a better hospital? He looked like the picture of health and managed to capture everyone with his magical smile.

This continued when we arrived on the Pediatric Neurology floor of the hospital. As they ushered us into our private room, Jack had all the nurses fighting for the chance to care for him. I'm sure it was partly that Dan and I were offering rounds of coffee (always needing to entertain), but I think most of the love was for our little man. He's always had a way with people.

Five more days of countless exams, tests, and romancing nurses (Dan with coffee, me with boyfriend advice, and Jack with his sweet smile) followed. We were starting to think that we would be sent home without our answer when the neurology fellow walked into our room. He asked if Dan and I could meet with his team to discuss some test results. Ten days earlier, I didn't know what a "fellow" was. Ten days earlier, I thought we were simply getting an MRI to rule out anything neurological.

Dan and I followed the fellow into a tiny, windowless conference room behind the nurse's station. It was a room I hadn't realized existed. At first, I was curious about this small room with a single sofa and scattered folding chairs, then I started to panic as I noticed the size of the "team." The room was too crowded. The fellow introduced us to the group—neurologists, BMT specialists, geneticists, and a social worker. Then he instructed us to sit on the small black sofa in the back of the room. Dan and I literally needed to walk over people to reach our destination. I kept thinking, *Why do all of these people need to be here? It must be bad news.* And it was.

We were told that Jack had Adrenoleukodystrophy (ALD). The worst-case scenario. As soon as I heard the word, I squeezed Dan's hand and excused myself. Again, I found myself climbing over people—this time trying to escape. I ran back to the room where Jack was waiting with my mother. I needed air. I paced around the room trying to calm my breath. My mother asked if we'd received any news. I nodded and ducked into the bathroom to throw up. As I rinsed out my mouth and glanced at the reflection in the mirror, it was like looking at a stranger. In ten days, I'd gone from a happy, fun-loving mother and wife to tired, anxious hospital mom.

My mother was standing in the bathroom doorway and kept punching me with questions. "What is it, Jesse? Have they figured it out? What's the treatment? Is Jack going to be alright?"

I couldn't speak. I couldn't bear to say the words. I wanted to collapse into her arms, but I couldn't. My child needed me—I couldn't be the child myself. Having no other choice, I left my mother and her questions without saying a word and returned to the meeting. I climbed back on the sofa, grabbed Dan's hand, and listened.

The doctors explained that ALD is a rare genetic disease characterized by the breakdown and loss of the myelin in the brain and progressive damage to the adrenal gland. It's caused by a mutation that is usually carried by the mother and affects only boys. There is no cure for ALD. Most boys die within two years of diagnosis. Most boys deteriorate quickly, losing their vision and hearing and ability to walk. They lose their ability to speak and swallow. They deteriorate until their brain cannot send the signals to make their hearts beat or their lungs breath.

We had two options. We could take Jack home. Enjoy life until the disease took over. Then we would "keep him comfortable" as his body destroyed itself. Or, we could choose a stem cell transplant. It is not a cure, but it could stop the disease from progressing. After hearing our options, Dan and I looked at each other and told the doctors to find a stem cell donor.

The doctors told us to sleep on it. They threw out mortality rates connected to transplant and explained the torture a body goes through even when it is successful. They told us that, in the case of some ALD boys, a transplant causes the disease to progress more rapidly than if nature takes its course. They told us to watch the movie *Lorenzo's Oil* (the 1986 movie following the story of Lorenzo Odeon and his family's fight to find a cure for ALD) and to learn more about the disease. Dan and I didn't need to talk or sleep on it. We'd known each other since college days and, while we might fight about which wine to serve with chicken or what color to paint the living room, we've always been on the same page with important things. We insisted that they needed to find a donor. We needed to save Jack.

When the meeting was over, Dan and I stood up and everyone stopped to shake our hands. Like the receiving line at our wedding ten years before. A strange gesture in light of what they'd just shared with us. The last person in the line was the social worker. She told us she was there for us, "whatever you need."

"Can you please write down the name of the disease?" I whispered. So powerless that I couldn't even spell the name of the disease that was killing my son.

She wrote it down on the back of her business card—ADRENO-LEUKODYSTROPHY. I held the card in my hand and tried to pronounce it. The word looked so complicated and so foreign.

That afternoon was the beginning of the ordeal of explaining. Endless phone calls and questions. Checking the Internet, then wishing that we hadn't. Frantic, but still needing to keep a smile for Jack. "No worries, buddy. We've figured it out. It's all going to be fine. Should we have Daddy grab us some Chinese food before he heads home to Anna?"

After dinner, Dan awkwardly hugged me goodbye. For ten days we'd taken turns going home to be with our daughter, Anna. We had friends and family helping us at home, but she was only six and needed one of her parents to tuck her in bed each night. We assured her that all this commotion was just until we figured things out. Now, both Dan and I knew that this routine would go on for a long time.

After Dan left, I snuggled with Jack, watching cartoons until he was asleep, and lay down on the blue vinyl pullout hospital chair that I had come to know well. The weight of the diagnosis made it hard for me to breath and the Xanax that the nurse had given me made my thoughts float.

I thought back to when I was first pregnant with Jack. I remembered what I used to say when people asked what I was having. Instead of the usual, "I don't care, as long as they're healthy." I would say, "I don't care, as long as they're happy." After all, what if the baby wasn't healthy? Would I love them any less?

Some people thought that they'd misheard, while others just thought I was being quirky. My own mother actually took offense. She felt that, as parents, our responsibility was to raise good people, defining 'good' as honest, strong, well-educated, well-groomed, and well-mannered. Happiness sounded irrelevant and too hippie for her. I tried many times to defend my hope. Happy people ARE good people. After all, don't you need to be honest and brave and strong to be truly happy? Besides, I wasn't sure if I could handle teaching the grooming or the manners or the state capitals (and certainly not spelling), but I did think I had a chance at teaching my children how to be happy. My mother and I would go back and forth for hours. We finally decided that, as mothers, we shared the same goal, just different words.

That first night of knowing Jack's diagnosis, I wondered if our family could still manage our goal of happiness. Was it possible to be happy after our world had been shaken? As I tossed and turned on the uncomfortable chair/bed, trying to imagine what our lives were going to be like, I worried that we might not even get through the next few months. Then I stopped myself. I couldn't fall apart. Jack needed me to be strong. Anna and Dan needed me to be strong. Falling apart would have to wait.

May 11, 2007

Dear Friends and Family,

As many of you may have heard, Jack was recently diagnosed with Adreno-leukodystrophy (ALD). ALD is a rare genetic disease characterized by the breakdown or loss of the myelin in the brain and progressive dysfunction of the adrenal gland. Our only hope to stop the progression of his disease is for Jack to undergo a stem cell transplant. Jack is home for a few weeks before returning to New York-Presbyterian Morgan Stanley Children's Hospital for the procedure. He will likely be in the hospital for 6-8 weeks.

You may want to research ALD on the Internet, but we must warn you to please be careful. Much of the information on the Internet is out of date and quite discouraging. We've set up this CaringBridge site to keep everyone in "the loop" with current ALD information and updates on Jack's progress. We're optimistic that the treatment his doctors are prescribing will halt the progression of the disease.

Obviously, this is a great shock, but we are staying strong and know that Jack will get through this with his sense of humor and beautiful smile intact. We thank everyone for his or her support and prayers and warm meals. For now, we are enjoying our time together as a family and gaining our strength for the battle ahead of us.

Love,

Jess and Dan

I was numb when I wrote those words. It had only been two weeks since Jack's diagnosis and I hadn't fully processed what was happening. Jack's illness is one of those things that terrify people. It either kills you or leaves you with a complicated life. Thanks to the Internet, within a week of learning the word Adrenoleukodystrophy, everyone in our lives was upset. Everyone was seeing the same information—a third of people don't survive a transplant, many boys end up requiring wheelchairs and feeding tubes, most ALD boys lose their hearing and/or vision during the process and the process is horrific, painful—absolute agony.

Our family had always been known for being fun. Our house was full of parties, Dan was a member of the local softball league, we were active supporters of our local schools, and as a photographer, many people knew me for my pictures. We were used to being approached with smiles and jokes, not tears and awkward hugs. With Jack's diagnosis, our identity changed quickly and completely. We were the family going through hell. We were the family losing their boy.

"Did you hear about Jack Torrey?"

"I read on the Internet…oh God, I don't know how they're going to get through this."

People have the best intentions and suddenly our family was surrounded by casserole dishes and prayer cards. And, there were the uncomfortable phone calls, the unpleasantly long conversations with acquaintances at the grocery store, and the statements we would hear again and again.

"God only gives you what you can handle."

"We are praying for you and your family."

"All things happened for a reason."

Not sure why people assumed that Dan and I would suddenly find God under the circumstances. We've never been religious. Not that we aren't spiritual, good people; we're just not huge believers in any particular organized religion. Our Sunday mornings have always been reserved for sleeping in and French toast. And, now that nature had screwed us, there was no way that we were going to put our trust in prayer. Modern Western medicine was where we were placing our faith. Dan and I had been married for ten years, and had our differences, but this was something we agreed on.

That's not to say we were completely honest with people. No "Why would a benevolent God torture our son?" Or "Don't bother praying—send money to myelin research." Instead, we would thank people and roll our eyes to each other. Dan was (still is) more frustrated with our charade than I am. He wishes people would just stop imposing their beliefs on us. I'm not a big fan either, but I don't feel quite as strongly. I'm not convinced that if we rack up enough prayers a miracle will happen, but all that good energy being sent from one human to another can't be a bad thing. Besides, what if they ARE right?

We only had 20 days at home between hospital stays, and spent much of our time bouncing between EEGs and blood work to last minute play dates and family dinners, trying hard to "enjoy this time together" as the doctors had asked us to do. We were playing the role for our kid's sake, and for our own survival.

One day, hoping to take a break from difficult conversations, we took Jack and Anna to our town's Spring Fair. Dan and I regretted the decision quickly as we dodged painful glances and teary people. We tried hard to focus on watching Anna get to giggle with her girlfriends and Jack wandering happily and obliviously around the fair with his buddies.

He was wearing an oversized Rolling Stones concert tee-shirt, one of Dan's pride and joys—something he'd saved since high school and brought out only on the rarest, most special occasions. Giving it to Jack that day was the first of many meaningful gestures directed to our boy. Dan was so scared and he was willing to do anything—give Jack anything.

Across the playground, I watched a woman approach Jack and start talking. I wondered if she knew who he was and what she was saying. I moved close enough to listen.

"Hey—where'd you get that shirt? It's pretty cool," she said.

Jack smiled, "It's my dad's. I still can't believe he let me wear it!"

"You're lucky! I saw the Stones that tour. They were AWESOME! Hey—maybe you'll let me buy that shirt from you…how does $20 sound?"

She looked over at me and winked. I didn't know her, but I liked her immediately. She was warm and open and real.

"Twenty dollars! Wow!" Jack was visibly torn. "That's more money than I've ever had, but I think my dad might get kinda mad. He loves this shirt. Even more than any of his other music shirts."

"Okay, but tell your dad that if he's ever ready to get rid of it, he's got a buyer."

As she walked away, I was overcome with emotion. Hit hard by the innocent, normal, non-ALDishness of their brief exchange. I wondered if she knew that Jack was going to the hospital soon, that he might never come home. The ease of her words allowed me to briefly remember our old life. Before our family was defined by a disease.

I've gotten to know that woman over the last couple of years and I finally asked her if she remembered that day. She said that she remembers it well. Remembers not knowing how to handle greeting us, until she saw the shirt. There was something so easy about making the conversation about music instead of the heavy reality we were facing. She still laughs as she tells me that she would still buy that shirt in a heartbeat.

A few days after the Spring Fair, the phone rang and I could see "New York-Pres" on the caller ID. I was shaking as I put the phone to my ear. There was no time for pleasantries: "Please tell me that you have a donor."

"Yes." That's all I heard.

It was time to pack our bags and prepare for the next step in our journey.

May 20, 2007
Day -10 (ten days pre-transplant)

We're enjoying our last 'normal' Sunday morning for a while. We're getting admitted to the hospital tomorrow and expect to be there for 7-8 weeks. Jack's really comfortable and in a great mood. In fact, I think he's enjoying all of the extra attention.

It's much more complicated for Dan and me. On one hand, we're ready to begin this fight. We know that a stem cell transplant is the only way we have to treat ALD and we have full confidence in our doctors and in Jack's strength. On the other hand, we're scared. Scared of what the next few months will bring. Scared of the suffering that Jack will go through. We've tried so hard to be strong since Jack's diagnosis three weeks ago (it feels like years) and we need to continue to keep our chins up and our heads clear. Jack needs us to do that — now, more than ever.

Anna also needs us. For those of you who live close by—when you see our Anna Banana, please give her an extra smile and maybe even a hug. Dan and I are doing everything we can to keep life as normal as possible for her, but it's going to be tough. This is going to be a long fight and we're going to need everyone to stay strong for us.

Love, Jess

Usually, when people are heading to the hospital for a stem cell transplant, they've had years to process their diagnosis. Often they're arriving for their "last hope" after months or years of chemotherapy and radiation. They've done their research and really understand what they're getting into. We had 20 days to prepare.

On May 20, 2007, we arrived at New York-Presbyterian Morgan Stanley Children's Hospital and moved into Tower 5, room 505, a simple and very clean room with a single hospital bed at its center. There was nothing particularly special about the putty colored space, but I was happy to see a leather sofa, which would double as a bed for Dan and me, and a desk. Children's artwork hung on the walls and we had a huge window overlooking Broadway. We also had a private bathroom. That seemed extravagant until we were reminded that it was a necessity—Jack would be in isolation. He would not be allowed out of room 505 and no one would be allowed in his room without gowns, gloves, and masks. All in all, the room was pleasant, quiet, tidy. As much sitting room as hospital room. Our home for the next 71 days (although as we arrived, we had no idea how long we'd be there).

We brought two suitcases filled with clothes, books, and games. We also brought sheets, pillows, and towels from home, trying so hard to make Jack as comfortable as possible. He seemed almost excited. He was the center of an adventure. After months of being yelled at and tested and punished, he was being loved and spoiled by everyone. I wouldn't describe Dan and me as excited, but we were eager to get started. More than ready to "fix" Jack.

Along with the suitcases filled with things from home, we brought our Torrey social skills, determined that everyone on Tower 5 would love our family, telling jokes and stories and offering coffee to anyone who entered room 505. We needed all of the nurses, doctors, and hospital staff to love our family. If they loved our family, they would think of Jack as one of their own. They wouldn't let anything happen to him.

That first day started with time for us to get settled and prepare for the events that lay ahead. My mother took Jack for a walk and our team sat us down on our leather couch/bed to discuss our plan—about specific pre-transplant chemotherapies to be used to prepare Jack's body, the transplant process itself, and the list of medications that would be administered along the way. We were also presented with a calendar of the estimated seven weeks we would be there.

There was so much technical information. I allowed most of it to go past me, figuring my priority was to be Jack's mother, his support. I would allow the doctors to be responsible for the specifics. The one thing I did hear was that we were starting at "Day -9."

"Minus 9?!? Can't we just start at Day 1? I can't cope starting less than 0!"

"Mrs. Torrey, it's customary that when you start the process for a stem cell transplant, you start at a negative day number. The negative days are preparation for transplant. 'Day 0' is Transplant Day—Jack's new birthday."

Defeated, I leaned back on our couch/bed and felt the weight of the nine negative days. I reminded myself that most people going into transplant were already weak, but Jack was perfectly healthy (except for the silent disease killing him). His doctors needed the nine days to break down his body completely. Nine days to administer enough poison to rip his body apart so that it could accept a foreign blood source.

I was distracted in my thoughts and hadn't noticed that our team had finished their orientation until Dan grabbed my hand to help me up. "Jess, it's time. They need to start administering the medication. Remember to keep this easy for Jack."

My mother and Jack suddenly walked in the door and I quickly pushed down all my worries and put on my smile, "Hey, little man. You ready? These ladies have some special stuff for you, then we'll have some ice cream."

Jack and his smile hopped on the bed, not seeming to notice the jumble of countless machines. He was too focused on the pretty blonde nurse as she hung the first bag onto his IV pole. "Hi, I'm Jack."

He had a central line in his chest (a broviac—three lines for IV medication to go directly in the bloodstream) that had been placed the week before. Dan and I watched as one bag after another was hung on the IV pole and then attached to our son. We had only been back in the hospital three hours. It was definitely less than zero.

May 22, 2007

Day -8

Jack started chemotherapy at 8:00 a.m. sharp. It was painful to watch as the IV bag was added to his ever-increasing tower of medicine. I tried to stay cool, but I must have asked Jack a dozen times, "How do you feel? Is your stomach okay?" He kept looking at me like I was nuts. The truth is that he was fine. Comfortable and happy. The two-hour treatment went by without a hitch.

The morning continued and so did Jack's list of medications. Jack still had a smile on his face, but he was starting to get a little bored. Lucky for us, in rolled my dear friend Kim with the biggest, most beautiful box of goodies. "Jack's Box of Fun" had arrived! I've seen Jack happy, but I don't think that I have ever seen him glow so brightly. Three hours after starting chemotherapy and he started singing "It's the Best Day Ever" (SpongeBob). Can you imagine? THIS was his best day ever!

I can't thank everyone enough for all of the gifts and cards and notes. Jack is thrilled, and Dan and I are overwhelmed by how lucky we are to have so many wonderful people in our lives. As for Kim-- you are the most amazing, creative and generous person that we've ever known. Thank you. We're so lucky to have you as a friend and Jack is so lucky to have you as a "Love Aunt."

Love, Jess

Our good friend, Kim, came into our lives fifteen years ago. We met at our block party shortly after we all moved into Maplewood. Kim and I instantly hit it off. We each had two children (a boy and a girl), husbands who loved sports, old houses that we managed to make sparkle, and the need for a good friend.

I quickly learned that she was a cancer survivor. She shared that she had a stem cell transplant. At the time, I knew nothing about the process other than that it sounded awful and that I was happy that she was alive and healthy. A couple of years into our friendship, she was once again diagnosed with cancer. That time I was with her and learned more than my share about chemotherapy and radiation and the hell of illness. Little did I know that she was providing me with an education I would soon need.

As soon as Jack got his diagnosis, Kim was there for our family. She'd sit with me for hours and listen to my worries and let me cry. She'd also let me laugh—never judging my mood. One day, she took Jack out for ice cream to tell him that she too had had a stem cell transplant and tried to explain to him what to expect. Another day she came over to take a family portrait, something we'd never done before (probably because family portraits were what I did for a living). But, after getting Jack's diagnosis, I was suddenly obsessed about getting the perfect picture of the four of us. What I told Kim was that we needed a picture to look at over the next few weeks while our family was scattered apart. She smiled and nodded. Everyone smiled and nodded a lot at us during that time. It was an attempt to keep from letting the thoughts slip out from their brains. No one wanted to share their fears, share that they were thinking that this picture might be our first and last family portrait.

As a children's portrait photographer, I always told my clients that the images that spoke to me were the ones where I could hear the laughter. Wrinkled shirts and dirty faces never bothered me, as long as I could hear the laughter. We still have the family portrait that Kim took that day in almost every room of our house and the laughter is absolutely present. Perhaps there's a hint of worry in our eyes, but you can definitely hear the giggles. Even now, for a child who can't speak, Jack sure can make a lot of noise with his laughter. Even in pictures.

After the portrait was taken, Kim continued to share. Although she was brutally honest about what to expect during the transplant, she didn't just share the hell of her illness with us. She also shared some of the beauty that her illness brought out in people. She shared stories of buying her wig with her mother and aunt and making a day in Brooklyn out of it. She shared stories of meals and letters and love that poured her way as she fought her battle. She also shared the story of her colleagues and the magical box they'd made for her. It was a box full of gifts from everyone from the CEO of their company to the garage attendants. "One day I'd open a beautiful bottle of perfume and another I'd open sweat socks. It was perfect." Every gift mattered. Every gift reminded her of how many people were on her team.

Inspired by the box that had been made for her, Kim started preparing a box of goodies for Jack as soon as we learned that he was going to need a transplant. A big cardboard appliance box was covered and painted with interconnecting arms "hugging the treasures." A poem was written across the top.

Jack's Favorite Things

Bright colored Legos stacked so high
And books of all sorts put a gleam in his eye
Whether jamming to IPOD tunes
Or simply watching his favorite cartoons
These are all things that Jack loves to do.
Star Wars, Spiderman and Pokémon are favorites too!

He loves his new pet Webkin
And let us not forget his crazy dog Finn!
Wearing his Yankee baseball hat makes Jack proud as can be
Because it makes he and his Daddy happy
Playing with Anna or getting hugs from his Mommy
Are tops with our special boy, Jack Torrey!
Family trips to NYC or simply watching a movie
Traveling is always fun as a Torrey
Especially when you visit cool places like Chile, Block Island,
and Disney!
A common sight to see, as those who live on Clinton Avenue \
would agree
Is Jack scootering along or bike riding with his buddies
All of these fun things make Jack simply happy!
Boundless curiosity and full of surprises
Little boys come in all shapes and sizes
Jack, you are no different with your fun loving style
That just thinking of you makes those around you smile!
Your friends and family have filled this box with some of your
favorite things
If this box could talk, it would have much to say
So instead, please read the many heartfelt wishes sent your way
And enjoy this great BIG HUG to let you know you are LOVED
Each and every DAY!!

The box also included instructions of how and when to grab a gift: "First when you wake up. Then when the clock strikes noon. Then, when you look out the window and see the moon." Friends from all over town contributed. Family from all over the country contributed. It was a huge box, literally filled with love.

For weeks Jack had been hearing about his Box of Fun and when it rolled into room 505 that first day of chemotherapy, it did exactly what it was supposed to do. It brought laughter and love. The Box of Fun quickly became a centerpiece in room 505. Three times a day, Jack would reach into his Box of Fun and pull out a treasure. Its home was under the TV, where Jack could look at it all day long.

On Day -1, Jack asked his nurse to help him retrieve a goody from his box. Eight days into the preparation protocol, and he was barely able to sit up. As she handed him the gift, Jack's doctor arrived with the news we'd been waiting for: Jack was ready for the stem cell transplant. His counts were so low that his body wouldn't fight the intruders that we were about to introduce to his bloodstream. We were all smiles as we heard the news. Odd, knowing that it meant Jack was so weak that a cold could kill him.

May 30, 2007
Day 0

We're going to keep this entry short and sweet. We're all exhausted. Jack had another remarkable day. At 1:00 p.m. he received his transplant. There were 15 people squeezed into room 505 and we all watched as "the Little Lady from Detroit" made her way into Jack. It took only 29 minutes (we didn't even get to half of our music playlist) and Jack had a smile on his face the entire time.

It was a huge day for all of us, but we are still at the beginning of a long journey. Keep those prayers and positive vibes coming.

Love, Jess and Dan

For those of you lucky enough to have never seen a stem cell transplant (when the cells have come from cord blood), it's not nearly as complicated as you might think. It's not a surgery; it's literally a small bag of blood—very magic blood—that goes into the vein like any other transfusion. It's done in the patient's room. Sure, there are extra doctors and nurses and monitors (including a crash cart), but basically it's a little anticlimactic.

We all sat and watched the cells flow into Jack's veins while listening to Dan's playlist and cheering for "The Little Lady from Detroit." Anna held her big brother's hand and we told jokes and magical stories about the little girl who was saving Jack's life.

Dan spent hours on the playlist before Day 0, including every artist he could think of from Detroit—music has always been Dan's therapy. "What do you think of the Supremes? Maybe that's too obvious. Maybe we should focus on the Commodores."

Thanks to Dan's playlist, we spent the 29 minutes that the cells went into Jack's veins singing and dancing and laughing. The staff wasn't too surprised by the playful mood in room 505 that day. They'd come to know us pretty well in the short time we'd been there.

We weren't the sad family, hiding and crying in their room—we were the Torreys. Always listening to music and entertaining visitors. And, when we weren't amusing friends and relatives, we were busy making friends with the staff. We knew about everyone's wives/hubands or boyfriends/girlfriends. We knew where everyone was from and what inspired him or her to work in medicine. Part of it was to pass the time and part of it was that we needed to make them feel like family, so that they would treat us like family. We were also just being ourselves. We'd always been festive around our children, and this would not be an exception. Now, more than ever, we needed to keep them laughing. Dan and I also needed to keep laughing. If we allowed ourselves to stop laughing, we were scared of what would happen.

As for "The Little Lady from Detroit", I'm not sure when we named the donor, but it stuck. Unlike bone marrow from a donor, an umbilical cord donation does not come with much information—just the blood data, gender of the donor, and the city of origin. All we knew about the cord saving Jack's life was that it came from a little girl, born two years earlier in Detroit. We wish that we had a real name and an address to send the family letters and love and cookies and thank-yous, but without a name, all we could do was celebrate it as a gift and have as much fun with it as possible (again, it's the happy in us).

The next few days were fairly uneventful. Jack was sick, but his pain was manageable. We watched TV, played video games and chatted the hours away. We'd convinced ourselves that we were one of the lucky ones. We'd say stupid things to the nurses like, "We hear that 5% of people don't lose their hair. I bet you Jack is part of that 5%. Right, Jack? You're going to keep that mop of hair aren't you?"

The nurses always smiled and said, "We'll see."

On Day +9, Jack and I woke up and as I was going through our new morning routine, I noticed his pillow looked dirty. Further inspection revealed that small hairs were covering the pillow and the back of Jack's head had a large bald circle. By the end of that day, Jack was completely bald.

That night, I took Jack to the bathroom for his nightly shower. He was starting to need a lot of help with this routine, a routine that was effortless for him just days before. I rolled the IV bar with one arm and supported Jack with the other. "Come on, little man. Just one step at a time. We can do this, JackO."

I managed to get him cleaned up in the shower, then to the sink to brush (or gently swab) his teeth. Jack was weak but still all smiles until he saw his reflection in the mirror. At first, I don't think he realized that he was looking at himself. But it only took a moment for his eyes to fill with tears.

That moment marked the beginning of hell.

June 13, 2007
Day +14

Yesterday Dan and I had to battle each other for the turn to cross out "Day +13" from our calendar. Things have gone from difficult to almost unbearable. Jack has had a feeding tube for a few days and it did not seem to want to stay in place. On top of that, his stomach was in an uproar, his mouth sores have worsened, and he needed to get the dressing changed on his broviac (the port which connects him to his tower of medicine, blood products, and nutrition). Jack's being a trooper, but his mood is being trampled by the pain and frustration of this process.

Today, Jack and I woke up to find two IV towers housing Jack's necessities. I don't know why I found this to be upsetting (all things considered). The poor nurse got the brunt of my hysteria. I demanded that we go back to one tower. "I don't care how you do it, but Jack is NOT lugging around two towers!" In retrospect, this seems a little irrational on my part. The truth is that Jack gets up once a day to take a shower, and maybe one other time to use the bathroom or to sit by the window. It is not as if "lugging" two towers would be difficult.

Lucky for us, the day improved. The doctors started Jack on pain medication and his mouth sores are settling down a little. His feeding tube was NOT reinserted (for the fifth time) and he is not missing it one bit! Jack is now receiving everything he needs through his veins—except for hugs, smiles, and jokes!

Thanks to Mymom (my mom), Dan and I are both home for the night with Anna. It is hard to be away from Jack, but we are really looking forward to a night together and time with our little girl. It's been over three weeks. Amazing how much we used to take for granted.

Love, Jess

P.S. — Jack only has one tower.

June 16, 2007
Day +17

Well folks, I sure hope that we have seen the worst of what this transplant has planned for us. The last two days have been the most difficult so far and I hope to never see a day like yesterday again. Jack started having stomach pain on Wednesday night and it got progressively worse until Thursday night when he was in agony. I don't use that word lightly—AGONY. For Dan and me to see our Jack in so much pain was heartbreaking. I can't begin to imagine what Jack went through.

Tests, tests, and more tests have ruled out anything too serious and Jack's pain is now well controlled thanks to the pain team and our wonderful nurses (have I thanked them yet? I will need to devote more than a line for that—maybe to-morrow). He and Dan are now both sleeping soundly. We are hoping that Jack's comfort continues and that he will start getting stronger soon.

Good news on the "count" front. Our doctors would kill us if they knew that we were sharing this news and getting "too excited," but what are the chances that they will see this...besides, TEAM JACK needs some good news. Jack's white blood count was 0.7 this morning (normal is 4.0 -10.9, but he has been less than 0.1 for weeks)!! "Cautiously optimistic that engraftment may be starting" is what the doctors said this morning. No promises, but "The Little Lady from Detroit" may be doing her thing! We're just hoping that this good news continues and that Jack stays comfortable.

Thanks for all of the support.

Love, Jess

Hair loss you expect. Nausea you expect. Exhaustion you expect. You don't expect the pain associated with growing bone marrow or the sores that can start growing in the mouth, go down the GI tract, and out the anus. You don't expect that being put into diapers is not only humiliating for an eight-year-old, but that the diaper rash can cause an infection that can't properly heal without an immune system. You don't expect having to have a nose tube reinserted several times a day because it keeps getting vomited out. You don't expect NEEDING a nose tube because your son can't swallow through the pain.

We kept thinking it would be over soon. We'd be teased by good days and mentions of going home and then we'd wake up to bad news. One day Dan and I spent in training to prepare for heading home — learning IV care and how to change Jack's broviac (his central line) dressing, and that night I helped wheel Jack down for an emergency CAT scan to find out what was causing such excruciating stomach pain.

It was 2:00 a.m. and I sat with Jack's nurse in the otherwise empty waiting room. She was holding my hand, telling me to stay strong. Her words were directed at me but her gaze remained straight ahead, which I found frustrating. I knelt down in front of her and forced her to look into my eyes, "When is this going to end? When is he going to start getting better?"

Still trying to avoid my eyes, she just shook her head, "Jess, I don't know. This is really bad. I'm not sure what's going to happen."

Startled by the words, I sat down on the floor. She'd worked on the pediatric BMT floor for four years and had lost many patients. It suddenly dawned on me that she thought we were going to be part of that list. It had never occurred to me that there was a chance that we wouldn't bring Jack home. I'd become a master of distracting myself from that reality. I allowed my thoughts to wonder for a moment, then I pushed them away.

I got to my feet and tried to stand strong. "Not Jack. Jack's going to be fine," I assured her. I sat back down on my chair and searched for another topic. "Tell me again about your date last night."

Allowing myself to focus on silly gossip and the brief moments of positive news is what helped me survive. It's odd reading these posts now—horrific stories followed by excited mentions of blood counts, of smiles, of songs. It's simply what I needed to do to function. Taking one moment at a time. Getting through the torture, but then allowing myself to enjoy any bit of good news that I could find.

It was like I had a switch that could go from panicked to relaxed. From concerned to totally optimistic. But after a while, the switch got harder to flip. Early on, I looked forward to Mymom (Jack's nickname for my mother) sending me home for the day or insisting on staying with Jack for the night. I longed for time away. Time for myself to relax and decompress. But after that night on the floor of that waiting room, I rarely left the hospital. Too scared of not being there.

I needed to control something during this time, so my daily routine became very structured. I would wake up each morning with the nurse change at 7:00 a.m. I'd shower, get dressed, and ask the nurse on duty to sit with Jack (still asleep) while I went for coffee. The coffee was only five floors down, and the nurses would often roll their eyes at my request. It was an errand that only took a few minutes, but I did not want Jack to be left alone. Once I had had my coffee, I would start getting Jack ready for the day. I would take him to the bathroom, sit him down on a folding chair in the shower and hose him off. I would let him stay sitting as I toweled him dry, got him dressed, and then brushed his teeth. Once he was clean and dressed, I'd get him back into bed. Then, we'd turn on the TV or read a book.

I wanted to be in charge of what I could manage as far as Jack's care, but I did look forward to the nurses coming in with medications and treatments. It was so much easier to pass the time hearing about boyfriend troubles than focusing on my little boy suffering in the bed next to me. Jack also seemed to enjoy his time with the nurses. He always seemed more comfortable when one of his "girlfriends" would sit down on his bed and gossip.

Poor Dan didn't have the luxury of sitting down and gossiping. He was trapped between two worlds. He would go to work and come to the hospital in the late afternoon. After an hour or two of catching up with us, he would go home to give Anna attention. He had to be able to flip his switch at a moment's notice. He had to cope at work, smile for Anna, and be strong for Jack and me. To this day, I do not know how he did it.

June 17, 2007
Day +18...Father's Day

Father's Day should never be spent in a hospital room discussing blood counts and hoping for a bowel movement (we prefer the traditional breakfast in bed and tie combination). Unfortunately, this is where we are, but we've tried to make the most of the day.

Dan and Anna came to the hospital bright and early, prepared to share a beautiful Sunday with us. Unfortunately, it was a tough morning. Jack's WBC (white blood count) was holding at 0.6 and the doctors seem encouraged, but our little guy was running slow. He couldn't talk, could barely sit up, and had so much difficulty walking that it took four of us to get him to the bathroom when nature finally called. Thank heavens Jack improved as the day progressed.

By this afternoon, Jack had drunk some water, pooped, and said, "Happy Father's Day." Water, poop, and words — sounds silly, but it was the best gift Dan could have received. Dan left the hospital with his other favorite child, Anna Banana, with tired eyes but a huge smile. As I watched them head towards the elevators, holding hands and talking about their dinner plans, I wished so much that Jack and I could join them. Jack hasn't left this room in almost a month.

Jack is fighting an incredible battle right now. His eight-year-old body has put up with more than most humans could bear. And, he's done this without complaint and even managed to keep his smile. I think that he's been able to stay so strong because of all the love around him. His father, Dan, is at the top of the

31

list of "Team Jack." Dan is the most devoted father I have ever seen and his love for both of his children cannot be rivaled. Thank you, Dan. I love you more every day—HAPPY FATHER'S DAY!!

We also need to recognize two other important members of "Team Jack." Ray and Juan (PopPop and Nonno) are both incredible people and loving fathers and grandfathers. They've been part of this battle from the beginning and continue to lend their support and love every day. Thank you. Thank you. Thank you. We love you more than you will ever know.

HAPPY FATHER'S DAY to all you other dads!

Love, Jess

P.S. Dan—as good as today turned out—let's go back to our traditional Father's Day next year!

We celebrated many holidays in the hospital that year. Each of them was especially depressing, as if a special day marked on the calendar further underlined our reality—our inability to truly celebrate. Father's Day was no exception. Jack was profoundly sick and Dan was suffering more than anyone realized. Spending each day going back and forth between the outside world and our hospital world was taking its toll. He was exhausted but kept to his new daily routine. He got up early so that he was ready to go work as soon as Anna's bus arrived. He went through the motions at work and then settled back into his car for the 40-minute journey to the hospital. Finding his way up to the fifth floor without needing to think, he would land at the door to Jack's room, pull a gown from the shelf, cover his then crumpled suit, and put on a mask and gloves before entering the room. As the weeks went by, I would see him pause for a second before he opened the door. Taking one last breath before putting on a smile for Jack.

I would greet Dan at the door and whisper any updates that I didn't want Jack to hear, before giving him his token kiss. I wore my uniform of yoga pants and a tee-shirt. There was no need for me to darn the gown and gloves because I was nearly as quarantined as our boy. Besides, the staff felt it was important for mothers to be able to comfort their children without the constraints of paper and plastic. The rewards outweighed the risks.

Having a sick child is hard for both parents, but fathers suffer in a unique way. Like the exemption from needing to wear gowns and gloves, mothers aren't required to hold it together. We are allowed (almost encouraged) to collapse. Daily visits from social workers, religious staff, even massage therapists, were constant reminders that we were delicate. It was okay for us to cry and vent, while most of the fathers I would see on the transplant floor held to the silent requirement to stay strong. I was so lost in my own fears that I couldn't see through Dan's sturdy facade. He always managed to put that smile on his face, but now I appreciate how scared he was and that, in some ways, he was mourning his son.

While Jack was still alive, we were starting to suspect that his life—and our lives—would never be the same. Dan's dreams for his only son were fading (or at least dramatically changing). His dreams of his son playing baseball and going to college were replaced with surviving and being able to walk. And, there were the fears that we shared that Jack might not survive.

We spent Father's Day in 2007 like every year, as a family. We had cake, told stories, and listened to music. We managed to make the most of it, but it's devastating to re-read my journal entry now. The past is sometimes harder to remember with the perspective of what the future will bring. In 2007, we were just going through the motions, as if we were only days away from returning to our former lives. We didn't realize that our future would never go back to days pre-disease. It would be a new life. We would adapt, and enjoy many Father's Days full of smiles and laughter, but Dan would never again hear his son say, "Happy Father's Day."

Sadder still is thinking about Anna during this period. As I've been sorting through the journal, I wanted to find what I'd written on her birthday in 2007. What I found was startling.

June 28, 2007
Day +29

I know that I have used this expression before (and that it is over-used in general), but the last couple of days we've been on a roller coaster.

Yesterday's WBC was 3.4 (normal is 4.5 — 10) and we were all elated. Dan and I spent the day with Jack and felt comfortable leaving to have dinner at home with Anna. We rarely get time like this with Anna and my mother (Mymom) offered to stay with Jack. Two hours after we left, Mymom called to say that I should get back to the hospital ASAP. Fever of 102.3—the nurses and doctors were worried about line infections, Graft vs. Host Disease, and a bunch of things that I've never heard of. Fortunately, he responded well to the antibiotics and he is much better this morning.

Now, for some great news—today, Jack's WBC is 4.4!! That's almost within the normal range!! Jack now has permission to walk the halls (as long as he wears a mask and has lots of assistance). Still no "home" date, but we are getting closer.

One more thing—HAPPY BIRTHDAY, ANNA!! We all love you very much!!

Love, Jess

"One more thing—HAPPY BIRTHDAY, ANNA!!" That's how I acknowledged Anna's 7th birthday. I honestly can't remember what we gave her as a present that year or if we even bought her a present. We did throw her a spa/sleepover birthday party the following weekend. I let her invite too many girls, allowed too much sugar, and had all of the mothers stay to help pamper the girls. In fact, what I remember are fifteen screaming 7-year-olds in tons of make-up and the moms sitting and drinking too much wine until all hours.

Everyone knew to ask about Anna while Jack was in the hospital. They knew it must be hard for her to watch her brother suffer and her family scatter each day. I knew enough to call her every night and I knew enough to sleep at home at least one night a week to be with her. But, when I'd go home, I'd mostly sit outside and enjoy the fresh air and the quiet. I'd allow myself to cry and call my friends to come over. I knew that Anna wasn't getting enough of my attention, but I couldn't give her any more. All of my energy went to helping Jack. I had nothing left for my daughter. I was ashamed of myself, but I couldn't seem to find the balance.

One night, Anna and I were sitting on the deck, sharing a big Adirondack chair. I was enjoying being outside and Anna was clinging hard to me. Holding on to her mama so that I wouldn't leave. We were talking about her day at the pool when suddenly she asked, "Mom, I miss you. Why are you always at the hospital?"

I took a deep breath. "I'm so sorry, baby, but I'm sometimes just too scared to leave Jack."

It was the only explanation I had. She knew that there was a possibility that Jack wouldn't survive (it was a conversation we'd been forced to have with her early on). She seemed to understand, hugging me, and telling me it was okay. We just sat on the Adirondack chair, enjoying the way she still fit on my lap. We were quiet for a long time, but I could tell the conversation wasn't over. Anna always fidgets when she's thinking.

Finally, she found the words she was looking for, "Will you stay with me if I need a transplant?"

There we were, sitting on our deck, hugging and crying. Just one summer before, the only memories on that deck were of parties and dinners and laughs. Now, sitting on that same deck, her question caught me so off guard that I was silent for a time. When I caught my breath, I managed to say the only thing I could think of: "Banana, you will never need a transplant. Only boys get ALD."

She kept looking at me, waiting for something. I sat lost for a minute when I realized that she needed to hear the words. "Yes. If you ever need a transplant, Mommy will stay with you."

July 4, 2007
Day +35

Happy 4th of July!!

We hope that everyone in enjoying a great holiday. Jack and I had a fun Bar-B-Q (thanks to Mymom and Nonno) in room 505. Jack didn't eat, but he seemed to enjoy the party and the rest of us sure enjoyed the food. He did sing a verse of "Crazy Car" — Naked Brothers. He hasn't been singing much lately. Hearing his voice is nothing short of magic these days.

Jack's blood counts are not cooperating today. He's also is fighting a rash and fever. I know that it sounds discouraging, but I promise that his spirits are up. Team Jack (specifically the doctors and nurses) just need to "tweak" his medicine. We are sure tomorrow will bring higher numbers, long walks, and maybe even another song!!

Love, Jess

We also want to send big congratulations to Team Torrey on Block Island — they won first prize for their float!! Jack is very proud and promises to help in next year's masterpiece!!

If you ask most families what their favorite holiday is, they would say Christmas or Thanksgiving. The more religious might say Easter or Yom

Kippur. The Torreys are a different breed. The Torreys love the Fourth of July! All of us cram into my in-laws' home on Block Island and spend a few days eating, laughing, and sometimes sharing a drink or four. We go on hikes and bike rides and enjoy the beach. And, for a few years, we made a float for the Block Island Fourth of July Parade. Not a little, unprofessional float, but an incredible work of art. Mind you, we often fought a bit over the design and the materials, and always had trouble with the costumes and deciding who was going to ride on the back, but making the float definitely added to the Torrey Fourth of July experience.

As the Fourth approached in 2007, Dan and I talked about how unfair it was for Anna to miss being with her extended family for the holiday—especially that holiday. Anna had already given up so much. For months, she hadn't had her mom volunteering in the art room or her dad throwing the ball with her after work. Our only family dinners were carryout in a hospital room. I begged Dan to take her to Block Island. I meant it…really. I didn't want her or Dan to miss it. I knew it was the right thing to do, even though I knew it would be hard for Jack and me.

If it hadn't been for Mymom's food and Jack's verse, I wouldn't have gotten through that day. Jack was missing so much and missing his favorite holiday was more than I could bear. Sounds silly considering what we were going through. Why was a family holiday/party so missed? I guess it's because it was something concrete that we were missing. I think we were also starting to realize that, even if we returned to Block Island with Jack, it was never going to be the same.

We did make a float the next summer and Jack got to ride on the back, dressed as a clown on the April Fool's Day Float. We had a good time, but we all knew it was different. The energy of everyone working together was gone. It's another thing that ALD stole from our family. I don't imagine we'll ever make a Torrey float again. It's not the same. It's better that we all sit in the crowd and watch. Watching is something we can all do together.

July 9, 2007
Day +40

A few weeks ago, we thought that today was going to be our release date—not
so lucky.

Instead, Jack had a CAT scan and an endoscopy/colonoscopy. His doctors need
to find out what's causing his stomach issues. They're most concerned with
the possibility that he may have Graft vs. Host Disease (GVHD). Rejection of a
stem cell transplant means that the host (Jack) rejects the graft (The Little Lady
from Detroit). GVHD is when the graft starts fighting the host. It can manifest
in awful skin reactions, destruction of the liver (the most dangerous), or serious
intestinal issues.

As always, Jack was a trooper, but he is feeling pretty low tonight. The test
results will be ready by the end of the week. Until then, we are going to work
on our walking and maybe even some talking...he said, "Hi Daddy," on Saturday and today he said, "I love you, Mommy." Today was a hard day, but hearing
those words made it bearable!

Love, Jess

July 10, 2007

Day +41

Great news this afternoon—Jack's biopsies came back and he does not have GVHD. Although it is usually treatable, GVHD is a complicated condition and we are very relieved to rule it out. Still no answer to why he is having stomach issues and a rash, but his doctors are working on it.

Now that we have ruled out the more complicated explanations for Jack's discomfort, we're treating the symptoms and getting him ready to GO HOME!! Nothing is set in stone, but we're keeping our fingers crossed. We hope that we can bring Jack home next week. I feel strange even sharing this news and Dan may get mad at me, but I cannot help but share it with Jack's team.

No walks or words today, but we have high hopes for tomorrow. If it were up to me, we would walk all the way to 26 Clinton Avenue, but we may need to settle for a few laps around Tower 5.

Love, Jess

July 13, 2007

Day +44

The roller coaster continues. After getting the wonderful news that Jack did not have GVHD, we were elated and started packing (seriously—I packed up most of the toys, videos, and clothes). Dan and I were convinced that we would be home within days. Unfortunately, Jack's body had other plans. He has been fighting fevers and stomach aches all week. Also, Jack's WBC has dipped as low at 0.3 in the last couple of days. The doctors have been testing and scanning and putting cameras in all sorts of places, but we still do not know what is causing his symptoms. It is frustrating and scary, but we know that we will figure it all out soon. Today he seems to be much more comfortable—we are hoping that this is the new trend.

Love, Jess

The stomach issue Jack was having was terrifying. Watching your child scream in pain and not knowing why it's happening and how to treat it is not just frustrating, it's torture. It didn't help that when we had arrived at the hospital, one of the nurses had hung up a large seven-week calendar on the wall in front of Jack's bed. Each night, Dan and I would cross out the days and look forward to the end. On Day +40, the calendar ran out of days, and so did our energy. Humans have an unbelievable ability to be strong under the direst of circumstances, but we all have a breaking point. The calendar ending was mine.

I'd become quite close with the nurse who had hung up that calendar 47 days earlier. I knew all about her love of the Yankees and her disastrous break up with her cheating boyfriend. We'd become friends, but that day she saw another side of me. "What the HELL is wrong with you? How could you lead us into thinking that we'd be going home by now? How could you not prepare us? IT's your fucking job!"

At first, she thought I was joking. I'd earned the reputation of having a sense of humor, even on the dark days. I'd used humor to mask my pain and make everyone around us as comfortable as possible—I'd been raised to deceive when necessary. This time I couldn't disguise my frustration and I watched as the nurse grasped my fury and her eyes grew wide and teary. "Jess, I'm so sorry. We always use that stupid calendar. It's just a gauge—it's not supposed to be an actual time-line."

I grabbed her hand. "I NEED an actual time-line! I NEED you to find me the right calendar!" I knew I was asking for the impossible and I started to crumble.

"I'll be right back," she whispered as she tore off her gown and left the room.

She came back within minutes with another calendar and started to take down the original. "No! Keep it up. Jack earned those days. We all did."

Shaking, she connected the new calendar to the bottom of the old one. The new layer was different color poster board—a constant reminder that we'd extended our stay.

By Day +44, Jack was in so much pain that we were petrified. The pain team finally prescribed enough medication to keep Jack comfortable, but it meant that he was basically unconscious. After several weeks of agony and screaming, Jack's room became eerily silent. I'd sit by his bed and watch his favorite TV shows—pretending that he was awake with me. I'd have conversations with him, even filling in his answers. Each night I would pull the leather coach/bed over to his bed so that I could sleep beside him. I needed to be close to him, to touch him, and smell him and feel him near me.

Being near Jack helped calm me a bit, but there was nothing relaxing about nights in the hospital. Waking up is yet another thing that no one prepares you for when you're entering the hospital. Transplant floors may dim the lights at night, but they never go to sleep. Jack had medication and fluids running into his veins all night and when they needed to be changed, a loud signal went off. Sometimes several times an hour an alarm would ring and I would need to get up, silence the alarm, and call for the nurse. And, because of Jack's stomach issues, I would often wake up to the smell of a bowel movement. Although the nurses assured me that they were willing to do the cleanup, I always tried to take care of it myself. My son was eight—he didn't need anyone but his mother cleaning his bottom.

Never knowing how much you will sleep or what you will wake up to is unbelievable. You're so tired, but you can't let yourself relax enough to get real rest. I was prescribed Ambien, but found that it made me too sleepy to function. I settled on a ½ a Xanax every night at nine o'clock. It relaxed me just enough to let me fall asleep, but allowed me to wake up and function if needed—and many nights, I needed to function.

Sometimes the signals wouldn't wake me but the nurses would. They needed to discuss blood counts and fevers and problems. One night our nurse woke me up to tell me that something was really wrong. Jack had a high fever and his stomach was distended. He was in incredible pain. She and the doctor had ordered a CAT scan. Not for the morning, but immediately—it was 3:00 a.m. It wasn't the first late night scan, but I was frantic, shaking as we wheeled Jack down the deserted hospital hallways in search of a scan and an answer. Hospital hallways are far too quiet late at night.

As we waited for the scan to begin, I held on to Jack as he lay on the stretcher. We had this routine where I would tell Jack to close his eyes and breathe.

"Close your eyes, Jack. Close your eyes and breathe. In and out—in and out. Go to Block Island. Feel the sun on your shoulders and hear the sound of the ocean. The waves go in and out. In and out. Smell the ocean air and hear the sound of the waves. In and out—in and out."

That night as I tried to calm him with our little routine, I found that I was doing it as much for me as for him. I was so tired and wasn't sure how much more I could take.

After the CAT scan, we got Jack back to his room and he settled down enough to fall asleep. I was finally allowed to crumble. I rocked back and forth on my leather bed that night, crying and bargaining with God. Trying to breathe, trying to "go to Block Island." Jack couldn't die.

He needed to get through this so that we could bring him home. We could deal with anything as long as we could bring him home.

We had gone from wanting Jack to get "fixed" to just wanting Jack alive. When Jack was first diagnosed, Dan and I talked and agreed we wouldn't settle for anything but the best for our son. We'd read about the horrors that ALD boys go through during transplant. We'd read about the skills and abilities they often lose, but we thought that we'd be different. We had better doctors, we had more supportive families, we had better recourses. We'd do better.

At some point, we realized that nature is stronger than doctors, families, and recourses. And, nature had other plans for Jack. Dan and I went from talking about Jack's return to our local public school and little league to how we were going to get a wheelchair in and out of the house and learning sign language. We were willing to do anything to bring him home and be a family again.

Thankfully, the results of that late night CAT scan didn't reveal anything serious, and just as mysteriously as Jack had gotten sick, he started to get better. His counts started going up, as did his spirits. We were able to wean him off some of the pain medication, which allowed a little more of Jack to reemerge. And, again, we started to prepare for going home.

July 17, 2007
Day +48

Good news from room 505! After a weeklong detour, Jack's on an upward trend. He had another round of scans yesterday and nothing was found that could be responsible for the stomach issues or the fevers. His fevers are now limited to one a day (around midnight—I think that he just wants to get a little attention from his nurses during the night), and his butt is starting to clear up. (Quick aside—do you think that Jack is going to be mad that I've shared his butt issues with so many people? Maybe I should delete all of these entries before showing Jack this journal). Perhaps the best news is that his numbers are starting to go back up—his WBC today is 4.0!!

Forget the numbers being the best news—the best news is that Jack is back! The last few weeks, Jack was so uncomfortable and obviously depressed. It was hard to get a smile out of him. This week he's so much more comfortable. He's sitting up, interacting, and laughing and smiling. It's a huge relief to all of us. We're not going to guess when our "launch date" will be, but I'm hoping that we are home before too long.

Love, Jess

July 19, 2007
Day +50

That's right, folks—it's been 50 days since the transplant and 60 days since we moved into room 505. We never thought that it would be such a long stay and we are very eager to get Jack home. His counts are really great (WBC over 12.0 today), but we still have a few things to take care of. Maybe we'll get to go home next week—maybe the following — we're really hoping to be home by Jack's ninth birthday (August 5).

Unfortunately, one of the things we needed to take care of before heading home was a little surgery. Jack had a G-tube inserted in his belly today. This is a more permanent feeding tube placed directly into his stomach. His doctors don't feel comfortable that he will get enough nutrition by mouth without one, and at this point, we are willing to do anything to get our boy home. The surgery was quick, but, as you can imagine, Jack is having a tough afternoon. Thank goodness for our pain team.

Although it's hard to see him go through another procedure, it's a necessary step to getting home. We look forward to getting through tonight and having a good weekend.

Love, Jess

July 23, 2007
Day +54

Sorry for not writing over the weekend. Jack had a difficult time recovering from his G-tube surgery and Dan and I didn't seem to have the time or the energy to write. If anyone is thinking about having a G-tube put into their belly, please be warned...apparently putting a tube through the belly does not happen without pain. Jack left for the operating room feeling good and strong and returned mad, frustrated, and in a lot of pain. It was so hard for Dan and me to see Jack going through yet more pain. But Dan and I didn't have much choice—Jack's nose tubes kept falling out and neither of us could picture learning to put them in ourselves. Also, Jack has not really eaten in two months and does not seem to have much interest now (although he did hold a bite of a bagel in his mouth this morning). Another benefit of the G-tube is that we can use it for medication. Jack has so much medicine he needs to take orally, and when Jack does not want to cooperate, he sure can be stubborn.

Thankfully, Jack's now feeling great and we are once again looking at the calendar and hoping that the end of our stay in room 505 is coming up. Jack's WBC was 26 this morning (too high really—time to take him off the Growth Factor). After nearly two months, he's finally comfortable again and starting to get up and around. His doctors are switching the last of his medications from IV to through the G-tube. Now, it's a waiting game.

Cross your fingers, cross your toes, light candles, say prayers, wish on stars, do a dance—no more fevers, no more procedures, no more WBC dips, no more pain—we want to go home!!

Love, Jess

July 29, 2007
Day +60

Finally, we feel like we can share this news — we're heading home tomorrow!!

That's right, after 70 days, we are taking Jack home to 26 Clinton Ave. He's doing really well. His counts are strong and he's walking with very little assistance. He still needs to be strictly monitored, and is on more medicine than I could have ever imagined, but his doctors think we're ready to take over.

I'm going to run now and finish packing, continue studying all our at-home instructions, and try to get a good night sleep. I have a feeling that sleep might be tough for a while...

Love, Jess

We were so ready to get home. Ready to get our lives started again. Ready to leave our doctors and nurses and loud machines waking us up at night. Ready to focus on things other than blood counts and pain medications. We were ready to be a family again. I was ready to go back to being a mother to Anna and a wife to Dan.

Packing room 505 was challenging. It's amazing how much can be accumulated in 70 days. Cards, gifts, lists of medications, and emergency phone numbers. Blankets and pillows from home. Books and DVDs. And, of course, the Box of Fun. A huge amount of work, but it was exciting. We were leaving this phase of our journey. Our fight was almost complete—or so we thought.

Just as I finished packing up our room, our social worker arrived and said that she needed to speak with me. It was the same woman who'd written down ADRENOLEUKODYSTROPHY on the back of her business card 100 days earlier. I'd never quite forgiven her for giving me the card that started this whole process, and now she was sharing other news.

We sat down on the brown leather sofa that had been my bed for the last 70 nights. She awkwardly held my hand and I sat with my back stiff and straight. "I want to share with you that many parents find the first few weeks of being home following their child's transplant to be the most difficult."

I pulled my hand away more forcefully then I meant to. "Most difficult how? How could home be more difficult that this?"

I was fuming. After knowing us for over three months, didn't she get that we weren't the average family? I shook my head, but she insisted, "Trust me. It's really hard. There's a lot to do and you won't have the support you've had at the hospital. You need to know that so that you can prepare yourself."

"It's not going to be like that for us. We're the Torreys. We have meals planned and friends and family waiting. We have the medication organized. We're strong. We're ready for this. Besides, we've just lived through hell. It can't get any worse."

She kept talking, but I stopped listening and got up to walk her to the door. I needed her to leave. We'd been looking forward to going home for so long, and I couldn't bear to hear anything negative.

Little did I know just how right she was, and what was in store for us.

July 31, 2007
Day +62

Jack is home!! We drove up to 26 Clinton Avenue and were greeted by a crowd—balloons, signs, and cheers!! Jack hasn't stopped smiling. He loves being home, adores his freshly painted "Star Wars" room, and seems to be getting stronger by the hour.

As for Dan and me, we're thrilled and really, really tired. I know that we'll find our rhythm, but (come on) with 17 different medications (most, given several times a day), IVs, G-tube...I still cannot believe that the doctors and nurses are trusting us with this.

Thank you all for your well wishes and support!! We couldn't get through this without all of you holding us up. We promise to continue to keep you posted on Jack's progress in Maplewood.

Love, Jess

P.S. We did go back to the hospital today for a check-up (only 20 hours after being discharged). Jack is doing great, so I guess we are doing an okay job so far...

I sounded so optimistic in this post, but reality was a little less cheerful. It only took a few hours at home to realize that our social worker had been right. Life at home was more difficult that we had imagined. We knew that coming home would be an adjustment. We knew that caring for Jack with all of his medications and appointments wouldn't be easy, but we really thought that the hard days were behind us. We also assumed that the future would mirror the past. In fact, the reality was that we returned home to an entirely different life.

As always, our friends and family carried us through. My mother and father (Mymom and Nonno) came to stay for a few days and Kim had rallied the troops. We were greeted with balloons, signs, and well wishes. As we pulled onto Clinton Avenue, the excitement was palpable. We were home! We carried Jack out of our silver minivan, placed him on the sidewalk, and Anna and Dan each held up an arm. "Victory!!" Then, we brought out the Box of Fun and everyone cheered. The crowd got silent as they watched us slowly help Jack up our brick steps. Jack was able to walk but needed a great deal of assistance. It was the first time in months many of our friends had seen him and I could see that it was hard for them to witness, but when he reached the top, we got another round of cheers. I was tempted to invite the party inside, but quickly thought better of it. It was more than Jack could handle. "We love you guys. Promise to come visit soon."

We left our friends on our front yard, and walked into our quiet house. We were walking into our new reality. We'd left 70 days earlier with a boy who was walking, talking, and fairly independent. He fed himself, bathed himself, and dressed himself. We returned with a very sick child. He had a central line in his chest and a G-tube in his stomach. He required 54 syringes of medication through his G-tube every day and three IV medications. He needed to be bathed and dressed. He went through at least 17 diapers a day. He needed to be helped up the stairs and required assistance walking. Someone needed to sleep in his room and he needed constant supervision all day long.

The first couple of days were tough, but Dan was home from work and Mymom and Nonno were there. Sharing the responsibilities made the duties manageable. It's when we fell into a normal routine that things started to get really difficult.

Dan had the "luxury" of going to work each day, which left me with the brunt of the responsibility. I tried not to feel resentful, but I couldn't help feeling jealous as he put his suit on and headed out the door each morning. I couldn't help feeling jealous that he didn't know all the names of Jack's medications and what company delivered the G-tube attachments. I couldn't help feeling jealous that he didn't have to know all of the emergency phone numbers by heart and every doctor and nurse by name. I couldn't help but feel jealous that he didn't need to fake the smile each morning for Anna as she left for camp.

Ten years later, I'm still the only one that holds the key to Jack's survival, but I no longer find it overwhelming. It's oddly empowering. The most important job of my life. I have a file I keep up to date with all of Jack's doctors and current medications, in case of emergency. Otherwise, I keep everything organized in my head and on my iPhone. I have plenty of help throughout the week and each person knows enough to get through their shift, but I'm the manager. It's not the job I ever would have selected for myself, but it's not so bad. My boss is quieter than most and the benefits are good. I also get to wear yoga pants most days, and bathing is optional.

But, those first few months after Jack got home were incredibly difficult for me. The responsibility of being in charge, the loss of personal freedom, the physical work, none of these things came naturally to me. People would say (and still say), "God only gives you what you can handle." I hate that phrase.

No God I could believe in would have chosen me for such a life. Before Jack got sick, I was Jesse—fun, loving, creative, NOT organized, determined, and selfless. Even when we first came home from the hospital, I could never have imagined getting used to this new life. I really thought it was temporary. I kept telling myself that this was an adjustment period. It would pass and get easier. I really thought it would be similar to when we brought our newborns home from the hospital—a few weeks of sleepless nights, a few doctors' appointments, a little extra work, and then we'd settle into our new lives. Unfortunately, after a few days it became obvious that I couldn't handle the new responsibilities and Jack was not a newborn. He was almost nine-years-old, 65 pounds, and had no immune system.

August 8, 2007

Day +70

The roller coaster continues—Jack went to his clinic appointment on Monday and ended up getting readmitted into the hospital. It's hard to share this with you all, but I think that I should be honest — I've always thought that telling the truth takes the poison out of a situation. The truth is that I made a mistake with Jack's medication. Dan and I have been tired and overwhelmed and tired (did I mention tired). We've been giving Jack medicine 8 times a day—48 syringes a day (which we are in charge of filling)...I'm a really good photographer and a decent mom, but maybe I am not cut out to be a nurse. I gave Jack the wrong dose of one of his medications and he had a horrible reaction.

Anyway, instead of burying myself in a hole, I chose to tell the world (or at least Team Jack) so that others will learn from my mistake. We can't mess around with Jack's safety, and we need to know our limitations and ask for help when we need it. So here it goes....

We are the Torreys of Maplewood. We need help with Anna. She needs a lot of play-dates and a lot of shoes. We need help with meals. We love cooking, but I don't think that we can make more than mac-n-cheese for a while. We need help with our crazy dog. And (obviously), we need help with nursing.

Love, Jess

P.S. We had nurses start last night and so far, Jack has not had any other 'episodes.' We expect that our next clinic visit (tomorrow) will go well.

Day +69 started out fine. Jack and I left for the clinic at 7:30 a.m. As we drove to the city, I felt prepared with my cup of coffee and our "clinic bag," which consisted of diapers, wipes, a change of clothing, and Jack's medication. We also had an overnight bag, which lived in the trunk of the car—including toothbrushes and pajamas (a bag we'd been told to have, but I had sworn we'd never need). Jack was happily sitting in the back seat. He was always eager to get out of the house and excited to see his nurses. I was amazed at how quickly we'd adapted to this new schedule—new life.

We arrived at the hospital before 9:00 a.m. and wheeled Jack through the maze of New York-Presbyterian Morgan Stanley Children's Hospital, until we reached the Seventh Floor—Children's Oncology. We were just starting to get used to the sad stares a bald child in a wheelchair gets.

We checked in and got settled in our room—initially stem cell transplant patients receive a private room to keep them from being exposed to any lurking germs. I sipped my coffee and gave Jack his morning medication while we waited to be seen. Jack seemed a little tired so I laid him down and turned on the TV. He quickly fell asleep and I enjoyed the few minutes of quiet to read the paper.

Danielle, one of our favorite nurses, came in to draw some blood. Both of us were surprised that Jack didn't stir. Although he was weak (only three months post-transplant), he usually reacted to any commotion, particularly involving a pretty nurse. Danielle and I agreed that he must just be tired, but after an hour, I started to get a little concerned and tried to wake him. I sat him up, put a wet washcloth on his forehead, and even sang (that usually got him excited). Nothing woke him. He was like jello. Literally, he was not functioning. I ran to get Danielle.

She tried all of her tricks—toe tickles and lights in the eyes—but nothing woke him. She called in the doctor. Within minutes, there was an army of people in our room running all sorts of tests. They kept asking about the morning routine and what medications I'd given him. One doctor asked in passing, "Are you sure you gave him the right amount of Adivan?"

I froze. I remembered giving Jack the Adivan, but did I give him the .25mls or 2.5 mls? I was silent. Trying so hard to reassure myself, but I couldn't.

I'd drawn the medication the night before. I'd set up our old butler's pantry as the pharmacy, full of lists and charts and even a mini fridge. I was proud of my newfound organizational skills. Jack needed 48 doses (8 different medications) each day. Drawing medication in batches was to make life easier. I had bins of syringes of all sizes. The largest was 20 mls—for the Mucomyst. And the smallest was 1.0 mls—for the Adivan.

Could I have used the wrong syringe? Could I have drawn the wrong amount? How much sleep had I gotten the night before? How much sleep had I gotten that week or that month?

I was lost in thought, trying desperately to remember how much Adivan I'd drawn, and was startled as the doctors called a code. Suddenly, Jack was on a stretcher. As we rushed through the hallways to the ICU, I had to admit my mistake. They needed to know what I had done. All my confidence and bravado slipped away and I was just a mom begging them, again, to save my son. "You've got to help him. It was too much Adivan. I gave him too much Adivan."

I was breathless as we arrived at the ICU. I sat down on the one small chair in the corner of the room, trying to stay out of the way as I watched the doctors hook Jack up to all the monitors. No one seemed particularly surprised that there had been a medication mix-up. In fact, they seemed almost relieved that it wasn't something more serious. And, they never scolded me, knowing that I was already scolding myself.

Now I appreciate that I wasn't to blame. I had no business acting as mother, wife, nurse, pharmacist, and driver. No amount of charts and lists and practice could have prepared me for this new life. How could I have managed it at all? How did I not refuse? Before we were discharged from room 505, I remember feeling that I had no choice but to go home and take charge. I'd watched other families leave the hospital and they didn't seem too overwhelmed. Now, I realize there was a huge difference between Jack and most of the kids leaving Tower 5. Most of those kids had cancer. Sick for sure, but they could mostly walk and talk and use the toilet. Most of those kids could help with their own care. Most of those kids didn't go home with brain damage.

Our social worker had warned us as we were leaving the hospital, "… it's really hard…You need to know so that you can prepare yourselves…" Now we were living it. We needed more help and the medication snafu had shocked us into the realization that things had to change. As soon as we got home the next day, we arranged for nurses to come to the house a few days a week to help. They helped us draw medication, care for Jack's G-tube and Broviac, and watched Jack so that I could run errands and nap.

Thanks to Kim, we also started accepting dinner every night. Although I loved to cook, not cooking provided me with an extra hour in the evening and limited my grocery shopping. She organized meals prepared and delivered by friends and neighbors. Each night at 5:30, I would check the cooler on the back deck. Lasagnas, fajitas, stews, even bottles of wine, would be left for us. It was another "Box of Fun" for our family.

Asking for help can be hard. There is something awkward about admitting that you need meals or groceries, but I discovered that everyone around us was anxious to help. It allowed them to be part of what we were going through—and part of the recovery.

With this newfound help, we started to get settled into our new life. I even started to feel old selves coming back.

August 21, 2007
Day +83

We had a great walk to the Maplewood Village on Sunday! Jack made it all the way to the ice cream shop (for those of you who are from out of Maplewood, it's about four blocks). Since Jack has not really been eating, neither Dan nor I thought about getting him any ice cream. It was Anna who filled her spoon and said, "Come on Jack—it's delicious!" Sure enough, sister knows best...Jack enjoyed most of Anna's bowl!!

Today, Jack and I made our way into the city for his clinic visit. Last minute, I put some snacks in the bag along with his daily medications and several changes of clothes—poor Jack has been known to go through quite a few during these visits. After giving some blood and changing his Broviac dressing, we sat and started our routine of 9:00 a.m. medications and looking for a movie to watch. I saw a bag of Oreos and I asked Jack if he wanted one. One, two, three...eight later, I called Dan and yelled, "Jack is eating!" I put the phone to Jack's ear so that he could hear his Daddy's congratulations and out comes, "Hello Daddy!"

Jack then proceeded to freak out his nurse by saying, "Hello Karen," and we made more calls to practice our new voice. "Nonno," "Mymom," "Pop Pop," "Nanna Sue," "Anna,"—no "Mommy" yet, but we're working on it!!

GO JACK GO!!!

Love, Jess

P.S. When we got home, I offered him a bowl of Doritos and fixed him some pasta. Not a chance. I guess that the "Little Lady from Detroit" has a sweet tooth!!

August 26, 2007

Day +88

We're still enjoying Jack's progress. He still seems to like Oreos and had some pasta last night for dinner. His word of choice is "Hi." We're still working on "Mommy." His doctors are also happy with Jack's progress. In fact, we only need to go to the clinic once next week!!

The biggest news is we've scheduled the Broviac to be removed on September 13th!! 19 days!! We'll be finished with our daily IV meds. Such a huge relief. No more worries of a "break in the line" or the dreaded "line infection."

Love, Jess

August 27, 2007

Day +89

Another good day. Anna got Jack giggling with her crazy sense of humor and out came some words… "Anna," "Awesome," "no," and "Jack" ("ack"). We've been so worried about Jack's speech, but the words seem to keep coming. We're so blessed.

Love, Jess

"The words seem to keep coming." We were so excited to hear Jack's voice and to see Jack eating. We thought it was the beginning of progress and the end of ALD.

Now we know that ALD often teases. Sometimes a brain signal can go through temporarily and haphazardly, never to return again. How? Why? What kind of disease is evil enough to steal communication? What kind of disease is evil enough to tease? It's torture knowing that the words were temporary, but I wouldn't take away the joy of hearing Jack's voice during those early days. We needed that joy to make it through.

Although some of Jack's early progress was just a tease, Jack has made some lasting improvements in the last ten years. Jack is eating now like the teenage boy that he is. He can't reliably feed himself, although sometimes I find him using a fork with unbelievable dexterity. Usually, someone sits beside him and feeds him like we did as a toddler. He still has trouble swallowing liquid, but we can trick him if we shove a pretzel stick in his mouth after giving him a sip of water. I expect someday he'll be able to drink on his own. His brain seems to be carving a new path. He's also able to hold a pencil again and occasionally able to write a line or a circle. We hope that with more occupational therapy, we'll see even more improvement with a lot of his fine motor skills.

Honestly, I would trade pencil holding for a few words in a heartbeat. The speaking is non-existent at this point. He hasn't sung in years and we haven't heard a single word in so long that I can't really remember the sound of his voice. I wish that we had appreciated his early talking moments even more. I wish that we had video taped them and been more careful to notice what prompted Jack to speak. We can't help but hope that it's not completely random. Somewhere under the ALD damage are Jack's words. There must be a trick that we are missing. We will always hold on to that hope.

It's that hope that got me searching for other boys with ALD. I kept thinking that if we could find other ALD boys, we might be able to crack the code of retrieving the words.

August 28, 2007
Day +90

All of the prayers and good energy that have been sent our way have been incred-ibly powerful. Thank you, thank you, thank you. I'd love it if you could all spend a minute (or many) sending some good vibes and prayers to the other boys with ALD.

Those of you who know me well may think it is funny that Jesse is starting a prayer group. I may not be too religious, but I know that all the love and energy that has been sent our way has helped us so much during the last three months and I think we should share the wealth.

After a desperate attempt to find other families fighting ALD, I've finally found a few. I was looking forward to having a support network that really gets what we're going through. I was also eager to learn strategies and techniques that might help Jack. Unfortunately, what I've learned is not as hopeful as I'd envisioned.

It's extremely difficult to hear what these poor boys are dealing with. Loss of hearing and vision are more common than anything. The inability to walk, swallow, and/or speak are also common. And, 'torture' is the only word that can begin to describe what it's like to go through a transplant. All this, and many of the boys haven't survived. ALD is brutal!

I've said it before, and I'll say it again—Jack is lucky. We all are lucky. Of course, the love, prayers, and positive energy have helped us, but these other families have been loved and prayed for, too. Life just isn't fair.

63

Please continue to send us your support and love and prayers, and also remember the other souls fighting this terrible disease.

I promise to be cheerier tomorrow.

Love, Jess

Even now, every couple of months I go on an ALD family-finding mission. I NEED to find other ALD families. Initially, it was to find the good stories. But, I quickly learned that there are very few good stories of ALD boys post-transplant. There are a few—if it's known that a boy has the "mutation," they are closely monitored with blood work and MRIs, and sometimes put on Lorenzo's Oil (a combination of oils which seems to prevent or delay the onset of the disease). If/when the boys do develop symptoms, the disease is caught very early and doctors can perform a transplant before too much is lost. These boys often do very well. Many return to their schools within a year post transplant, and return to their lives without too much complication.

Unfortunately, unless doctors are looking for the disease, most boys don't have the luxury of an early diagnosis. Like Jack, most boys are misdiagnosed (usually with ADHD), until they've lost enough to really alarm their parents and doctors. Most ALD boys have started to lose their vision and/or hearing, and those that haven't before transplant often do during the process. Either before or during transplant, most boys also lose their ability to walk and swallow.

Many boys with ALD post-transplant are partially or completely blind and deaf and can't walk. To make things worse, most boys don't lose anything intellectually. They completely understand that their bodies are failing. They're trapped in a body that doesn't work. They're trapped and they can't yell for help because ALD also steals their ability to talk.

Early on, I would seek out ALD families, hoping desperately to find something positive. I would sit for hours on the computer, thrilled when I'd find a family, then devastated when they would share their story. Most boys had lost their fight after months or years of torture. Others were left with very limited lives. I could picture these boys, once living typical lives, now either gone or trapped in a bed with machines feeding them, suctioning them. They were often blind and deaf, unable to speak. These boys had lives so complicated and uncomfortable that it's hard to not wonder if those who died weren't better off.

It took years to appreciate that Jack is a success story. For years, we were lost focusing on what he couldn't do. Even now, he can't feed himself (unless he is presented with a pile of cookies, which he manages to devour without hesitation) or consistently swallow liquid (requiring him to still have that tube in his belly to administer hydration — the tube we had thought was temporary). Jack is also very dependent when it comes to everything from dressing to toileting to walking down the street. His dependence demands similar attention to that of a two-year-old. But, even with his complicated life, he is able to do quite a bit. He can walk and see and hear. Things most people take for granted, but those of us in the ALD world know are luxuries. And, Jack is happy. After so many years living this new life, we realized that we have indeed been blessed with happy children. That dream we had, even before our children were born, came true. It might not be the life we envisioned, but we need to appreciate that our biggest goal has been accomplished.

With newfound optimism, I now seek out ALD families to share something positive. "Lucky" is not a perfect word to describe Jack's experience, but he's certainly more fortunate than most of his peers, and I seem to use that word often. "Jack's so lucky. He's really doing great." I sound like I'm talking about my teenager as he applies to college when in fact I'm chatting about something as simple as his progress with toileting.

Parents who have just received the dreaded diagnosis are either appalled by my relaxed attitude or relieved to hear a mother making jokes, "Yes. Jack still has his G-tube. I don't really see any point taking it out. In fact, I wish I had one to make my wine consumption easier." I'm just trying to find some humor in keeping the tube that we need to leave in Jack's belly because he can't swallow effectively enough to remain hydrated throughout the day. Focusing on the positive, I've managed to distance myself from the negative as much as I can. After all, this is our life, we might as well enjoy it.

As I talk to other ALD parents, I need to remember that Jack's disease is rare, even for ALD. Jack's ALD started in his frontal lobe (usually ALD starts in the back of the brain). Unlike most ALD boys, his hearing and vision don't seem to be affected (although it's hard to be sure, because he can't communicate). He's also lucky to be able to walk and we've even retrained his swallow reflex enough that he can swallow food.

We do, however, think that Jack has lost more intellectually than most ALD boys. Sounds strange but we're not sure it's such a bad thing. He's lost just enough of his intellect so that he doesn't seem fully aware of how hard his life is. He's rarely frustrated or angry. He never focuses on what he doesn't have or can't do. He has lost just enough of his smarts to simply focus on the moment and to focus on being happy.

It's Jack's positive mood that keeps those around him positive. It's contagious. Jack has set the tone for our family and we fall in line. Anna remembers little of what life looked like before ALD and shares her brother's attitude. If both of our children are living without complaint, how can Dan or I complain? Now, even mornings when I'm greeted with a messy situation (usually involving poop), I'm also greeted with Jack's electric smile. As I lift his 100-pound body into the tub, he puts his hand on my shoulder and continues smiling. As I put the sheets into the wash, he walks in circles around me, happy to be alive. And, as our dog tries to eat the mess left on the floor, Jack laughs and laughs.

September 8, 2007
Day +100

The doctors tell us that this is not really such a significant day, but let's face it—their kids have never gone through a transplant. We are so happy to reach this milestone. The last hundred days have been difficult, but we have gotten through it. And, we've reached this day with Jack home and feeling strong. I have given my last dose of IV medication (thank heavens) and we are getting the broviac out next week. We have so much to celebrate!!

Thank you all for being part of our journey. Thank you for the meals and the notes and the gifts and the calls and most of all for the love that you have showered on us. We cannot imagine having gone through this without each of you.

Jack is relaxing now, recovering from a fun night with his grandparents. Tonight we are going to the Marshall Ice Cream Social. If there are any of our doctors or nurses reading this—the party is outside, Jack will wear a surgical mask, and we will not let anyone touch him.

Love, Jess

P.S. The MRI we did last week of Jack's brain went well. A little progression since the transplant, but his doctor is not overly concerned.

Day 100 is a day that people going through transplant look forward to. The myth is that if you make it to Day 100, and you are fully engrafted, you're home free. The truth is that we've known many people who have suffered plenty after that date. And, we've known a few who have died.

But, when you are going through the hell of a transplant, you need something to reach for. Initially you reach for numbers—blood counts, engraftment percentages. Then you set your sights on going home. Once home, you dream of freedom and you hope that with Day 100 you will earn a little independence. The ugly reality is that Day 100 comes and goes with very little fanfare. Jack still needed a mask to leave the house. A mask along with a diaper bag and a change of clothes.

So that's what we did. We put a mask on our boy, threw a diaper bag and a change of clothes in the car, and headed to the Marshall School for an ice cream social. We missed so many of Anna's activities over the last six months and this seemed like an easy outing. It wasn't until we pulled up to the school that I felt my stomach start to tighten.

I was sitting next to Jack in the back seat of our silver minivan. My father-in-law was busy talking to Dan in the front seat and Anna was chatting with my mother-in-law about the latest High School Musical movie in the third row. As we approached the school, I glanced over at Jack and saw as his eyes registered where we were going. It was a mixed expression of excitement and confusion. I realized that Jack hadn't been back to the school since we had taken him out for a simple MRI five months earlier. So much had changed in those five months and I started to panic about how Jack would react to seeing his former classmates and teachers.

We found a parking spot in the crowed lot and I got out of the car, suddenly feeling very apprehensive. As I walked around the minivan to get Jack out of the car, I started to regret our outing, "Dan, maybe I should stay in the car with Jack. This might be too much for him."

"We're here, Jess. We gotta do it." I could tell from his tone that Dan had his reservations, but he was right. We needed to do this. With Dan's help, we got Jack out of the car and started to head down the path to the mass of familiar faces.

Kids ran around the playground with ice cream stained faces and adults crowded a table filled with coffee and cookies. Everyone was busy catching up, back from their summer adventures. At first it seemed that we would be allowed to slip into the crowd without any disturbance, but then I noticed as people glanced in our direction and suddenly the voices softened.

Several people stepped away from the crowd to approach us and I could tell they were as uncomfortable as we were. Arms hesitated before they hugged and no one knew what to do with Jack. After all, he did arrive with a mask, which clearly indicated that germs were an issue. "How about a high-five?" was my quick solution to the situation.

The flurry of greetings was sweet, but the awkward exchanges made me glance at my watch more than once. How quickly could Anna gobble down her ice cream? Was a half hour enough to prove our love to her? Jack enjoyed the attention and didn't seem to notice the tear-filled eyes of his teachers. He simply stood, holding my hand, and smiling at everyone who approached us. Even now, Jack is much better at these situations than we are.

As soon as I saw Anna swallow her last bite of ice cream, I nodded at Dan that it was time to go. I thanked everyone and started to guide Jack back to the car. As we walked away, I could feel all eyes were on us and wondered how long it would take for the atmosphere to return to normal. I hated that our family could affect a mood so dramatically.

As we got back into the car, Anna asked again and again why we needed to leave so quickly. My mother-in-law tried to take the blame saying that she didn't feel well and needed to lie down, but Anna knew. "It was because of Jack. It's always because of Jack."

Anna was in second grade and even her ice cream social had been taken over by Jack and his illness. I tried to reassure her that things were getting better, but we all knew that it was unlikely that we had seen the last of ALDs complications. Just five days later, we would get another reminder.

September 13, 2007

Day +105

After a long day at the clinic, we are in the ICU at the hospital. Jack and I went to the clinic yesterday expecting a long stay (a few hours) because he was due for his IVIG (a bi-monthly med). What we did not expect was chills, fever, and blood pressure problems. We went from the clinic to the ER to the ICU.

Thankfully, Jack had a good night—or as good a night as one can have in a loud ICU covered with wires and monitors. He has a line infection, but it is responding nicely to the antibiotics. I cannot believe we made it until two days before his central line was scheduled to be removed... Anyway, now he is having it removed tomorrow and they will install a temporary line in his arm so that he can get IV antibiotics. His doctors expect us to be here a week or two. We thought Day 100 meant we were done with overnight stays, but it looks like we are going to spend a little more time on Tower 5.

Poor Dan had just landed in Texas when he heard the news that Jack was getting transferred to the ICU, but managed to get a flight back and is with us now. We are going to take turns here at the hospital so that we can make life as normal as possible for Anna. My parents will need to hold things together at 26 Clinton Avenue this week, but we know they are up for the task. As far as Jack is concerned—he's doing great. His energy is still a little limited, but he is happy to see his old pals. Jack has missed all his nurses and doctors!

We are lucky all this happened while we were at the clinic. I cannot imagine having seen him go through that while we were at home...Again, I use the word "lucky"—who am I kidding? This stinks, but we will get through it. I'll keep you posted.

Love, Jess

The timing was remarkable. Day 100 came and gave us a tiny hint of freedom, but as soon as we found some comfort and stability, ALD needed to prove it was still strong. It was scary at the time, but I did not fully appreciate how serious a line infection can be. In retrospect, I know that the line infection was as close as Jack ever came to dying. A central line provides a direct path to the bloodstream. With Jack's fragile state, I am not sure his body could have fought off the bacteria quickly enough. Had we been at home when the infection started, it's likely he would not have survived for the ambulance to arrive.

The morning that the infection happened began like most days in the clinic. We arrived around 9:00 a.m. and got settled. Jack's nurses flirted with him as they weighed him, checked his vitals, and then they began their routine of taking blood and flushing Jack's lines. I was a little distracted that morning because my brother, Pablo, was visiting from Florida. My brother and I hadn't always had the closest of relationships and I found that visit particularly awkward from the start. I was busy trying to make him comfortable, offering him coffee, and introducing him to the nurses and doctors. He was showing off some tricks he knew on Jack's wheelchair—I'm still unclear as to how he knew how to do wheelies with a wheelchair. We were acting more like he was visiting me at my dorm in college than my son's room at the clinic.

It wasn't until I heard Jack's nurse swear that I realized there was a situation. I looked away from my brother balancing on the back wheels of the wheelchair like a prepubescent boy, and back to Jack's bed. The nurse looked flustered and upset and reached up to hit the red button. EMERGENCY. "What's going on?" I asked as I jumped out of my seat.

"Step back, Jess. He's having a reaction. There must have been some bacteria in the line."

Within seconds, the room started to fill with doctors and nurses. My brother and I were ushered into a corner as we watched them pump Jack's body full of one medication after another. Jack's body was seizing and he seemed to be developing hives. Pablo seemed uncomfortable, not knowing where to look and what to say, "I don't know how you get used to this stuff, Jess."

The idea that my brother thought this was normal almost made me smile. He had no idea what was normal to us, just that our normal was very different from most people. I considered letting him wonder, but thought better of it. "This isn't normal. Something's really wrong."

He hesitated, clearly not knowing how to respond. "Sorry, Jess. Maybe we should go around the corner and grab some coffee? This looks like it might take a while. And, I'm guessing this is hard to watch," Pablo said in a way that didn't make me upset, but did make me feel sorry for him. After months of living in hospitals, I'd seen more than my brother could imagine. My comfort hadn't been a consideration in a long time. Pablo had always been my older, smarter, more accomplished brother. Now he seemed naive.

"I need to be here, Pablo. Jack's going to need to go to the ICU. A line infection is serious." My lack of emotion was the only way I could say the words. Although I didn't know exactly what was happening, I was nervous because I'd heard the doctors call a "code." I had heard the "code" called from our neighbor's room on Tower 5 just months earlier. I'd seen the doctors and nurses rush into the room and heard the commotion build, followed by a disturbing silence throughout the floor. Everyone had been told to stay in their rooms, but I'd seen from the window of our door as the howling parents were ushered down the hall. That was the last time I saw that family.

Trying to push that memory aside, I turned to the gang of people surrounding my son and got swept into the mass. I'm not sure what happened to my brother that afternoon. He just disappeared, like so many things had that year.

Jack and I spent the next two days in the pediatric ICU and the next two weeks on Tower 5 recovering from his line infection. By then, I was no longer the darling of the moms on Tower 5. I'd become a bit of a pain in the ass for the staff. I didn't have the energy I'd once had for coffee runs and boyfriend advice. I asked way too many questions and made way too many demands. "Jack needs his steroids after he eats AND he needs a different sort of breakfast. I don't care if that means you need to call down to the cafeteria again."

I'd been managing Jack at home for a while and knew what was best for my boy. I also think I'd hardened a bit and didn't want to be part of the Tower 5 family anymore. I just wanted to be home.

I still can't believe that of all people, it was my brother, Pablo, who was with me during such a dramatic day. As adults, we had not been very close and he barely knew Jack. I think it was a business trip to New York and a guilt trip by my mother that landed him at the clinic that day. I was thankful he was there for the distraction, and I think that day ultimately made us much closer. I realized how much I needed him in my life, and he had a chance to see his little sister in a new light. Since we were small, Pablo has been the successful child—the best student, tremendous athlete, lucrative career. My younger brother, Phil, has been the rebel—the film-maker, the lacrosse player, the fun one. I'd been the child who everyone liked, but no one really admired. A mediocre student, a JV athlete, pretty enough to date, but never the prom queen. It took my child almost dying for my family to see that I am amazing at something. I'm a good mother and I am strong.

Dec 24, 2007
Day +207 Merry Christmas!

This Christmas obviously holds a special significance. I was racking my brain the other day trying to remember last year's holiday. Where were we? What did we do? I couldn't remember it. Dan had to remind me that we were in Chile last year. I nearly fell over. Of course, I remember our lovely trip to Chile. Friends met us there and my folks and brother Phil were there too. We spent time at my parents' house and we traveled around and lapped up the sun. We swam, ate, and drank plenty of good Chilean wine. It was a great trip, but was it really only a year ago? Jack was talking and playing and writing and reading. He was a typical eight-year old boy. Sure, he was showing some signs that something was going on, but we had no idea what the year would bring.

As we begin the holiday season, I'm torn between celebrating and cursing. I will start with the cursing so that I can end on a high note. How on earth did this happen? Why us? What did we do to deserve this? How are we going to get through the challenges of our new reality? We were the perfect family. Dan and I had a great marriage. We come from wonderful families. We had a lovely home and 2.5 kids (I count Finn as .5). We had more friends than any family deserves, and good jobs and financial security, blah, blah, blah. Perfect—really. Now things are so different.

Now, I will celebrate. As I look at the list I have just written, things are not so different. It's just that we have an addition to our family—and this addition has changed our lives so dramatically that it defines all of us. BUT, we still have a good marriage, exceptional families (who have risen to a challenge only few are asked to face), a lovely home and 2.5 kids (although Finn is walking a thin line right now). We now have even more friends and jobs (we have added nurse, administrative assistant, and child advocate to my list of job titles). Most of all, we have Jack. And, although he has changed, he is still our boy. He may not be able to talk to us or go to school or read a book, but he is still the same kid. He has a smile that speaks volumes. I said in my original note to everyone, "We are staying strong and know that Jack will get through this experience with his sense of humor and beautiful smile intact." He has managed to keep that beautiful smile and we will continue to stay strong and optimistic.

So let's choose to celebrate!!

Merry Christmas everyone!

Love, Jess, Dan, Jack and Anna (and even Little Finn)

Holidays are always an opportunity for reflection and this first holiday season following Jack's diagnosis/transplant was particularly raw. The juxtaposition between this year and its predecessor was extraordinary. Just twelve months earlier, we'd managed a thirteen-hour flight and went to a foreign country where we visited family and traveled around without much planning or concern. Granted, my father is Chilean and we've spent loads of time there, but it is still not as simple as traveling within the States. Just a year later, family travel seemed like a distant memory. We were even anxious about our doctors traveling for the holidays and we were stocking up on medication in case bad weather snowed us in for a day.

Our entire lives had changed in a year. Our goals, perspective, and priorities had all been forced to adapt to our new reality. A reality that included feeding tubes and countless doctors, but it also included the knowledge that we were surrounded with love and support. And, we were incredibly aware of how lucky we were to celebrate the holidays as a complete family. The dark days in the hospital just months earlier had taught us how fragile life is and to appreciate every ounce of what we had.

We enjoyed that holiday season and as we started the new year, we continued to work on establishing our new normal. I found more people to help me with Jack so I could escape some of my nursing duties and return to many of my old routines. It felt great to get out of the house with only an iPhone tethering me to Jack's health. I knew that his caregivers could find me quickly if a fever started or he had a fall, and I felt that sudden changes in his health were now less than likely.

As Jack's health became more stable, we realized that it was time to start thinking about him being able to return to the world. The usual recommendation is to wait a year following a stem cell transplant before going back to normal public interaction. A year is usually how long it takes for the body to build back its immunity. Jack's system seemed to be building quickly and by the spring of 2008, his doctors started talking about the possibility of school. At first I pictured him returning to his elementary school, but his new challenges brought me quickly to the realization that he would require a special school. Our hope was that it would be a temporary accommodation until he managed to regain the skills that ALD had stolen from him. As we approached the anniversary of his diagnosis, my new mission became finding the right placement for him. The search, like the anniversary, proved to be an emotional challenge.

April 30, 2008

Day +336

Today has been a mixed up day. A grim anniversary, but a positive step toward the future. Today is the anniversary of Jack's diagnosis. One year ago, our neurologists at New York-Presbyterian Morgan Stanley Children's Hospital sat Dan and me in a small room and told us that Jack had Adrenoleukodystrophy. We had two choices. The first choice was to bring him home and make him comfortable while his body quickly deteriorated. He would probably be gone within a year. Or, we could put Jack's small body through a stem cell transplant. The doctors and social workers talked about "palliative care," "chemotherapy protocols" and "mortality rates." Dan and I sat, hand in hand, and took in as much information as we could handle. People have asked if it was a hard decision for us to make. The truth is that it didn't feel like much of a decision. Dan and I only had to glance at each other to know what we needed to do. We needed a transplant. We needed to have hope that Jack could live.

So, that was a year ago. It's hard to remember that day, but life needs to go on and today we feel like we are starting a new chapter. For a few weeks, we've been looking at schools for Jack, and we think we've found a great candidate! While I liked seeing some of the other schools, as soon as we walked into the P.G. Chambers School I felt like we were home.

All the classrooms were full of kids with all sorts of challenges working, smiling, and laughing. I literally cried when they welcomed us into a classroom with,

"Look guys—Jack is here. Jack, come meet some new friends." The kids crowd-ed around to greet Jack and he looked so happy—truly beaming. He got an opportunity to sit with the class and participate in a couple of activities. It was clear that he is more than ready for school and to have more time with peers (and perhaps less time with his mama). So, Team Jack, cross those fingers and toes, light those candles and say those prayers. We think that we have found the school!

I leave tomorrow for the fun gals weekend. Mymom (my mom) will be here to help out and Dan has his list of "to dos" (not that he needs any lists). If anyone sees my little family this weekend, be extra nice and give them a hug for me!!

Love, Jess

Looking at schools for your child is always complicated. As parents, we want to find the perfect fit. Often perfection means that the school will provide the youngster with challenging academics or perhaps a strong athletic program. Sometimes a school search is an attempt to remove a child from a difficult or dangerous social situation. Just like all parents, when we were searching for schools for Jack, we were looking for the perfect school. The difference was that our definition of perfection was unusual and it took a while for us to get comfortable with our new defi-nition.

Our school district had sent out teachers to tutor Jack during his time at home. When they first met our boy, lying on the couch only wearing a diaper and a tee-shirt (I was exhausted by laundry and often just avoided extra loads by limiting the lower half of his clothing—he was nine—I was lazy), Jack was being fed 24 hours a day through his G-tube, so he was unable to move around too much. His team of teach-ers was wonderful and pretended not to notice his impediments, but they quickly set aside the third grade curriculum that they had been assigned. Instead, they would sit with Jack and read or tell him stories. It was only a few times a week, but I loved Jack's tutoring time. Just ninety minutes, but it gave me enough of a break that I could safely shower or nap.

As Jack approached his first transplant anniversary, his doctors agreed that his immune system was strong enough to return to school. I was excited to get back to a routine that felt normal and to get some time off from being in charge. I called the school district to find out our options. Clearly our team of tutors had shared their experience at the Torrey house. Our newly assigned case manager told us that Jack would require an "out of district" placement. "We don't feel that the Maplewood Public Schools can adequately educate Jack considering his current," long pause, "limitations."

I was not surprised by the news that Jack needed a special school, but it did concern me that she was convinced that Jack's situation might be more permanent than we had hoped. I swallowed my tears and started a flurry of questions about how to move forward. I was told that Jack fell into the category "Other Health Impaired" (a catch-all term for the children that don't have a clear diagnosis) and that he would require a school for the "Multiply Handicapped."

The term caught me off guard and I couldn't help but give this woman a hard time. "I know I'm new to all this, but I thought our kids were 'differently abled' or 'challenged'. 'Multiply handicapped' seems like an extra insulting term."

She hesitated, clearly looking for the right words. "Mrs. Torrey, you are absolutely correct. This term is a bit outdated. I will bring it up with the chair of the Special Education Department."

"Special—that's a word I've always liked. Let's say we are going to look at programs for the 'Multiply Special,'" I said, trying my best to sound light so that she could breathe again. I've always had the habit of trying to make jokes out of uncomfortable situations. It sometimes makes people feel EXTRA uncomfortable. We finished our conversation with me thanking her (using my lame "multiply special" joke again) and her faxing me a list of potential schools.

I poured through the list, wondering where they hid these schools for the multiply special. Why hadn't I ever seen them, or had I seen them and simply not acknowledged them? I looked at the brief descriptions and realized, living in New Jersey, there were more options than I imagined. I started my research, much like the year before, on the computer, looking up student/teacher ratios and academic information. Instead of athletic programs, I looked up information about physical therapy, occupational therapy, and speech therapy. I also made sure that we would only consider schools that had both an art and a music program. Jack was missing out on a lot, but he was not going to miss out on his two favorite subjects.

Once I was prepared with a list of several realistic contenders, I sat down with Dan and discussed the possibilities. I always tried to avoid boring Dan with too much of the research end. Even now, Dan is on a "need to know" program—it's too overwhelming and not completely necessary for him to be part of every detail. Besides, I like Dan to be able to focus on the fun of being Jack's dad.

So, once I had the list narrowed down, Dan and I decided that our priorities were a clean and safe school, equipped with not only a friendly staff but a program that would help Jack progress. Ideally, enough progress to get him the hell out of the school. Of course, we never shared our ultimate goal with our case manager. There is an unspoken rule when you are the parent of a child with special needs—you can never be openly repelled by your child's challenges.

Once we had a list of four or five schools I went on several tours with our case manager. I wanted to pare down the search even further for Jack and Dan. I'm glad I did, because the first few visits left me in the car crying, as my fears of our future became sharper. Knowing that Jack was part of this community of children with such complicated challenges was heartbreaking when I finally faced seeing his new peers. Even more frightening was when some of these schools said that Jack was not a good candidate for their program. I would look around at these broken children, startled that my child was more broken. Like all parents, it was hard for me to really see my child and his imperfections. It was still too early to be honest with myself, but I wasn't given a choice.

P.G. Chambers School was the last of our school visits and I decided to bring Jack and Dan, hoping that it would soften my reaction. As we walked through the corridors of P.G. Chambers School, we were all impressed by the facilities and the bright smiles and eager spirits that greeted our family. It was still difficult to maneuver through the halls, but I kept a smile glued to my face and worried that it looked forced. I wondered if everyone could see that tears were filling my eyes when I looked at Jack's future classmates. Although the program seemed perfect, the students at the P.G. Chambers School were more physically disabled than many of the schools I'd toured. I scrutinized the wheelchairs and walkers, wondering if I could have handled immobility on top of Jack's other challenges. I tried not to stare, but I was overwhelmed by some of the children with significant deformities. Jack's disabilities were hidden under a façade of a beautiful looking nine-year-old boy. Most of the children at P.G. Chambers School were not able to disguise their conditions and I couldn't help but find it a little disconcerting. I watched Dan have a similar reaction, loosely covering his emotions with his salesman's smile and polite nods at the information shared by the vice principal as she showed us around. Jack, however, didn't seem to be bothered by his peers' disabilities. He seemed so happy to be with other children and eager to join them. Like all children, Jack seemed to crave time away from his family.

Despite all of the disabilities apparent as we walked through the halls, Dan and I noticed that the children were together in the classrooms, while being cared for in a very individual manner. We knew that was what Jack needed. ALD post-transplant is a very rare situation and we required a team of people who would approach Jack with enthusiasm and create a program that would work for him. We left the school and told our case manager to send in the necessary paperwork. We wanted Jack to go to P.G. Chambers School.

The thirty-minute drive home was full of lively conversation, Jack smiles, and bright moods. We had crossed another thing off our "New Life List." Each of these milestones was getting us closer to our goal of living again. We were starting to accept that life would not return to where it had been before, but that it might not be such a bad existence. After all, the four of us were doing it together. If Jack could smile his way through, we all could.

At the end of my post to friends and family, I slipped in the mention of a girls' weekend. I was reluctant to share the news, feeling like I was abandoning my family, but everyone in my life was insisting I go. As the first anniversary of Jack's transplant approached, my girlfriends began planning a weekend away. I had been so buried in our new life that I hadn't realized that we had missed our annual fall girls' trip. It was a trip that five of us had taken for years—our time to soak in the sun and allow our husbands to change the diapers. I tried to tell them to go without me, but they wouldn't consider it. They talked to Dan and he agreed that it was a good idea—I needed a few days off and he needed to prove that he could handle things on his own. Mymom offered to help and I left them with a ten-page list of schedules, medications, and doctor's information.

I got on the plane to Hilton Head, thinking that I would turn around as soon as we landed, but instead I poured myself a drink and got lost in some fun girly conversations. We laughed for two days and I got to remember that I wasn't just Jack's mom. As the first anniversary of Jack's transplant approached, I was starting to realize that finding Jesse again was necessary to my survival. Perhaps even necessary to our family's survival.

May 30, 2008
Day +365

Jack has two birthdays now. August 5th 1998, Jack was born healthy and strong. He came into the world beautiful and perfect except for one little mutation. On May 30, 2007, Jack was reborn. This time combining with stem cells (the Little Lady from Detroit) to save his life. Both days will always be marked in my mind as joyous, incredible days AND days full of pain and exhaustion. I know that as a mom I am never supposed to mention the birth of my children as anything but spiritual and beautiful, but let's face it, childbirth is no picnic. Although last year I was not responsible for pushing or going through a C-section, the physical pain was intense. We watched Jack receive those precious cells and had so many expectations and so many fears.

We sat in the room with fifteen people watching the transfusion. Without turning my head away from the bag of cells, I asked our nurse practitioner/transplant coordinator, "When can we throw the party?" (Meaning—When do we finally get to celebrate? Is it day 30 if the chimerism shows engraftment? Is it that magic day 100?).

She put her hand on my shoulder and said, "It's gonna be a while. Maybe a year?"

Dan and I thought for sure we would be able to celebrate sooner, but would definitely celebrate the year anniversary with the biggest party that the Torreys have ever thrown (and us Torreys are pretty good at throwing a party). We planned to celebrate Jack and to thank all of you for your support by filling you full of food and wine. We planned to rent out the biggest venue and celebrate for a week. We were thinking rides for the kids and a band for the adults. What we did not know was that this first year would be exhausting. The idea of throwing the big party now is a little intimidating. We promise the Jack Party will happen and you all will be invited. Until then, we are going to enjoy Jack and his smile.

HAPPY BIRTHDAY JACK!!

Love, Jess

Honestly, I wanted to punch the nurse practitioner in the face when she answered my question with another question, "Maybe a year?" It's brutal watching your child suffer, but you can manage if you know when it will be over. You can cross off the days as you head towards the finish line. But, like the calendar that had hung in our hospital room, no one really had an answer. She wanted to manage our expectations and must have thought a year was a good, safe date. I'm sure she thought that it was a positive thing, giving us an answer. She may not have realized that she revealed her lack of confidence with her use of the word "maybe."

I tried to ignore her ambiguity and focus on the year, but it quickly set me into a panic—a year!! How on earth could we watch and wait and worry for a year?!?! Each day felt like an eternity, but we did it. A year after Jack's transplant, he was stable and ALD seemed to have weakened its grip on our boy. But Jack was still weak, so we waited one more year, just to be safe. Then, we threw the biggest party we've ever thrown. Until then, we turned our attention to other new beginnings: like school.

July 8, 2008
Day +405

Today Jack started at the P.G. Chambers School! As we walked through the doors of the school, I was a basket case. Sure, Jack has started new schools before, but never as a fragile, non-verbal, post-transplant boy. In our old life, I easily trusted almost anyone to keep an eye on my kids (truthfully, I may have been a little overly trusting), but now I am very careful. As we walked in for drop off, I had to remind myself again and again that I had to do it. As a friend said to me this morning, I was not letting him go, I was letting him fly.

I brought Anna with us. She was looking forward to seeing her brother's new school and I needed a little support. We lingered a while as Jack settled into his new classroom. His classmates are charming and welcomed him with open arms. His teachers and aides all seem to be incredible people and it was reassuring to watch as the morning routine got started. Although the school day is modified for the various challenges of the children, the day is similar to typical school. They started the day with one of the children holding the flag and the kids saying The Pledge of Allegiance. To my amazement, Jack mouthed every word!! It brought tears to my eyes and a lump to my throat. He is ready for his new life and ready for his new school. Anna and I chatted the whole way home about how wonderful the school seems.

Jack arrived home a couple of hours ago (I let him take the bus) and his backpack was full. Curious, I took at peek and was faced with the First Day of School Pile—you moms know that pile of forms and lists and sheets. He even had a homework sheet (seriously, I wasn't ready for homework). As I worked through the pile, I saw a sheet titled, "What We Did Today." I was delighted to see that his activities included art, yoga, and computer time. The note also included how many bathroom trips he made and how many diapers he went through—a little reminder that things aren't totally typical.

Thanks for all the well wishes and support.

Love, Jess

I will always remember that first day at P.G. Chambers School. Jack was dressed meticulously, with his hair (which had not been cut since it had grown in after his transplant, and often looked dangerously like Art Garfunkel) combed down with enough gel that it couldn't move. I packed the same backpack that Jack had used in second grade and filled it with diapers/wipes, a change of clothes and a healthy lunch. Anna questioned me as I packed that lunch, "Mommy. Jack doesn't eat brown rice and vegetables. Mommy—he doesn't really eat anything."

But there was no stopping me. I needed the school to know that Jack was a boy who was loved and taken care of. He might not eat this macrobiotic/gluten free/organic lunch, but it was available to him. And, he had a mother and a sister who were going to drop him off this first day and watch him as he got settled. I would not be the mother who tapped her feet waiting for the bus to arrive in the morning and singing "hallelujah" as it pulled away—that would wait at least a couple of days.

Ultimately, Jack spent five years at P.G. Chambers School and it became Jack's home away from home. It also became a safe-haven for the rest of the family. It was one of the few places in our lives where people understood us. Initially we did feel a little like intruders as we walked through the hallways. Most of the students had been attending the school (or a similar school) since they were little—early intervention in NJ often starts within the first two years. Most of these were children born with their challenges. And their challenges were profound. After all, they were not there because it was their neighborhood school; they were there because they have "multiple disabilities." Not just one severe disability, but several.

Initially, when I would visit the school, I found myself referring to Jack's classmates by their disabilities, "I saw Jack was hanging out with little Sally in the huge wheelchair." Or "Small-head Kathy sure eats a huge lunch. I saw her inhale half a sandwich in one bite." It took a little time, but I slowly noticed that the kids just became kids. "Lively Sally" and "Funny, hungry Kathy." I no longer defined them by their challenges.

It also took a bit of time for the P.G. Chambers School community to get used to us. Parents and aides were eager to introduce themselves, recognizing us as new to the school. When they would ask what school Jack came from they always seemed startled by the answer: "Jack was in our local public school in Maplewood."

I would see their confusion and add, "Jack didn't get sick until about a year ago."

This only added further confusion. These were parents that have children who were severely disabled, but many of them had never known a child who BECAME disabled (especially as old as eight). I ended up having more than one discussion with a parent who told me how sorry they were for me. That it must be so difficult for our family. I would accept their hug as I would look down at their own child in a wheelchair with a feeding tube poking out from under their shirt. I remember one conversation where a mom and I actually argued about whether it was harder to watch your child lose their words or to have never heard your child's voice. She thought that the memory of Jack's voice must be torture for us — that she couldn't imagine the weight of that memory. I argued that it was those memories of Jack "before" that kept me positive. After all, at that time I was sure that we'd return to "before."

Those conversations did become less frequent as the community got to know us. And, while those early exchanges were difficult, they did bring me close to the other parents. You develop relationships quickly when you're sharing such personal details. And we did a lot of sharing. Often simple things like doctor recommendations, but sometimes conversations got much deeper. We would sit for hours talking about fears for our children's future, fears for our marriages, and worries about our other children. Exhausting, but a necessary part of adapting to our new life. Many of these women will be friends for life.

At fourteen, Jack graduated from P.G. Chambers School and started high school. We went through the same sort of adjustment period. He now goes to school with teenagers and young adults and seeing these larger kids brought up a lot of anxieties about having an adult child with special needs. It's different having an older child who is unusual. It's harder to slip through a store unnoticed with a teenager holding your hand and it's harder to explain their quirky behavior. "Sorry he didn't mean to spill the cans. He forgets how fragile these arrangements can be." Or the really awkward, "Jack doesn't have great boundaries. He didn't mean to grab your bottom."

Having an older child with disabilities also means that Jack's classmates are all bigger and literally their challenges are bigger—bigger wheelchairs, bigger diapers, bigger people—with boobs and facial hair. Sometimes I've confused a student with a teacher. Once asking an attractive young woman where I could find the cafeteria and she answered by grabbing my hand, licking it, and trying to lead me. Another time, I introduced myself, using a very loud, slow voice, "I'm Jack's mommy. Are you new to the school?"

The young man gave me a funny look and answered, "Yes. I'm Jack's new occupational therapist."

These types of situations are further poof that two schools and almost ten years in, and I have not completely mastered this new life.

Jul 30, 2008
Day +428

Hi all,

This is Dan providing the update today... Today our family made our pilgrimage to Yankee Stadium. Jesse asked if I would write today's entry, and I gladly took the reins. You see, today was not just an average day for a Yankee fan....

I could give you the Reader's Digest version, but that just wouldn't be right, now would it? To put this visit to the Bronx in the proper context: this was Jack and Anna's first ever Major League baseball game; their first ever Yankee home game; the last year in the glorious 85-year history of the "old Stadium"; oh, and the Yanks had just lost 3 games in a row in the middle of a tight pennant race... so you got the picture?

We arrived very early — around 10:30 a.m. for a 1:00 p.m. start. Amazingly, the Stadium was already packed with fanatics — everywhere... We met our Yankee "Guardian Angel", Connie, outside the Press Gate, and we started our adventure. Connie led us through the gate and down some secret stairway to the bowels of the Stadium. We walked along a series of tight, crooked hallways with low ceilings and peeling paint, and photos of Yankee greats plastered all over the walls. This was surreal. Like being in a movie. We were really INSIDE the Cathedral!!! We took a sharp left and starting walking down a ramp. The floor was covered with worn astroturf. A blue hand-painted sign with white lettering hung

95

overheard. "I want to thank the Good Lord for making me a Yankee." — Joe DiMaggio. Connie told us that Derek Jeter touches that sign before every game for good luck "as he is walking toward the dugout." I touched the sign as I walked under it. That was cool. Wait a minute! Holy COW! Did she say dugout?! We're heading toward the Yankee dugout!!!! Suddenly we could see daylight through an opening ahead. We walked up three steps and took a right, and there we were — in the Yankee dugout.

It was a beautiful, hot July morning. A few players and a lot of staff and security were assembled on the field. The Orioles were stretching out, playing soft toss and getting ready for batting practice. We sat on the bench and took it all in. The Yanks were still in the clubhouse. Paul O'Neill walked by and said hello. Paul O'Neill!!! I shook his hand and introduced him to Jack and Anna. He signed a ball for them. Mike Mussina walked by. Moose!!! He stopped and posed for a few photos with the kids. Anna played shy and Moose teased her about it. Jack just stared him down. (Since Jack does not speak with his mouth, he speaks with his eyes instead...) So, he gave him the Jack stare... Moose stared back... A real Mexican standoff. It was like Moose was on the mound and Jack the slugger was trying to figure out whether he was gonna throw him a fastball or the dreaded knuckle curve. Moose got a kick out of Jack's tough guy approach. We were all thrilled. Dan Giese (reliever) said hello and signed the ball for them, too. We wished him luck this season. Dave Robertson (reliever) walked by. I would have asked him to sign the ball, but I was not totally sure who it was exactly (he is a rookie.) I did not want to embarrass him by calling him Joe or Steve or "Hey Rookie Guy in the Bullpen." So we took a pass.

Connie said that we could go up on the field and walk around in the designated areas. (We could not go on the grass because the players were practicing there and they want to avoid little kids (or dads) getting hit by errant throws, etc...) But we walked around on the perimeter and soaked it all in, and took a LOT of photos... The House that Ruth Built. It never looked better. I told Jack and Anna that Babe Ruth had sat in that dugout and played on that field. And Lou Gehrig, Red Ruffing, Tony Lazzeri, Bill Dickey, Joe DiMaggio, Yogi Berra, Casey Stengel, Phil Rizzuto, Mickey Mantle, Roger Maris, Elston Howard, Billy Martin, Whitey Ford, Bobby Murcer, Thurman Munson, Reggie Jackson, Ron Guidry, Graig Nettles, Don Mattingly, Paul O'Neill, Tino Martinez, Bernie Williams, Joe Torre — and don't forget George Costanza!

We lingered in the dugout for a while. Connie said most of the Yanks would likely not take BP today, because they had played a late game last night and it was optional, so maybe we would not meet any more players. Then her boss, Jason, came rushing over and said, "Come with me now." So we all rushed back up the ramp toward the clubhouse. We stood outside the clubhouse door in anticipation. Joba rushed by on his way to the pen (he is one big dude). Suddenly, the door opened, and Derek Jeter appeared. Derek Jeter!!!!! The Captain!!!! I wish you all could have seen the look on Jack's face. He nearly fell over. We all did! We asked him to sign the baseball, and pose for a photo with us. Jesse was literally shaking as she took the photo (now I think she is FINALLY a REAL Yankee fan! ;)). He asked where we were from. I said, "Maplewood, New Jersey — which is where Derek Jeter was born. Right, kids?" He gave me a puzzled look. So, I corrected the statement. "I meant you were born in New Jersey. Besides, Maplewood isn't that far from Pequannock." At that point, he gave me that, "Oh, so you're a stalker?" kind of look. No big deal. I've seen it before... Anyway, we wished him good luck this season, and told him we would be rooting extra hard for him today. Words cannot adequately describe how cool that experience was—a real once-in-a-lifetime thrill for all of us.

Connie then led us back to the dugout, where we got to meet the Yankees manager, Joe Girardi. He was great. He sat on the bench and took some shots with Jack and Anna. Then he said, "Connie, I have to stay here and get ready for the game. Why don't you take these guys up to my office and show 'em around."

Was he kidding???? Joe Girardi's office!!! The Skipper!!! So we went to his office and posed for goofy photos while sitting in his chair behind his desk. It was definitely cool. (He had an English muffin with peanut butter for breakfast — still half-eaten and sitting on his desk....)

Connie took us upstairs and showed us around the press box area. We met the Yanks PA announcer, some reporters, the "Official Scorer," and we even saw Michael Kay, Paul O'Neill and John Flaherty doing the YES pre-game show in their booth. Totally cool... We saw Mr. Steinbrenner's box, and we also got to pose for a photo standing next to the Yanks 2000 World Series Championship Trophy. Wow! She even showed us George Costanza's office. What a thrill!!!

Finally, Connie led us to our seats—Main Reserve—behind home plate and in the shade. Perfect!

The game summary: Joba pitched another gem for 6 innings — and he didn't even have his best stuff. The Yanks crushed the O's by a score of 13-3, avoiding a sweep. Bobby Abreu hit two homers and A-Rod hit another one out. The "Rookie Guy in the Bullpen" pitched well for two innings, and Dan Giese closed out the 9th to preserve the win. Jack and Anna got a big win for their first-ever Yankee game. Popcorn, hot dogs, loud fans yelling all around them (like Dad). Not even much traffic leaving the Bronx!!! Now, THAT is unbelievable...

And to top it all off, during our drive home, Uncle Matt called and told us that the Yanks had somehow made a deal to trade Kyle Farnsworth to the Detroit Tigers for catcher Ivan "Pudge" Rodriguez. (The guy only has 13 Gold Gloves, but he can hit...) So Jack and Anna (and Jesse) may get another chance to experience me experiencing yet another Yankee postseason run this year. "Ya gotta believe!" (Sorry, Mets fans...)

Go Yanks...

(EDITOR'S NOTE: do not be alarmed -- the Jacktorrey CB site will now return to its regular blogging content.)

(One last Editor's Note: at press time, the Sox are losing to the Angels by a score of 6-2.) Yippee!!!!

Love, Dan

A dear friend had worked for months to arrange this trip to Yankee Stadium. We were so lucky to have friends and family always looking to provide our family with an adventure and knowing our family, she knew that there is no bigger Yankee fan than Dan Torrey. The Make-a-Wish Foundation provided us with a trip to Disney World the following fall. We will always refer to our day at Yankee Stadium as "Dan's Make-a-Wish Trip."

Dan still carries the picture of our family on the field in his wallet, and we all carry the memory of that day in our hearts. I'm not the Yankee fan that Dan is, but that day made me understand the love of the game and the team in pinstripes. Everyone welcomed us with open arms and made us feel like part of the team. And, everyone seemed caught in Jack's magic spell.

At the end of the game, a few of the players looked up at where we were sitting. They pointed at Jack and gave a thumbs-up. Dan and I looked at each other in disbelief and then we looked over at our boy. He sat with his glorious smile, but didn't seem surprised by the attention, as if he had something to do with the win.

These huge days will always be remembered, but sometimes it was the smaller days that would have gotten lost without our CaringBridge blog.

I was startled to read a quick post written later that summer from when we were vacationing on Block Island.

August 23, 2008

Day +452

While riding by Rodman's Hollow this morning, I slowed down to take in the view. "Magical" is the only word to describe how the light hits it and creates a thousand different shades of green. The greens against the blues of the ocean — the image is breathtaking. On the far right side of the view, I noticed a little tree. Not a great looking tree. Not big or pretty, just a little tree. I thought, Wow—what a lucky tree. He gets to soak in that view all day, every day. He gets to live right here as the seasons change and storms move in and out. He gets every sunset and every sunrise. Of course, this got me thinking of Jack and the fact that he too is not the strongest tree, but he is getting to have a pretty magical view.

As you may have guessed, we're on Block Island enjoying the sun, the ocean, the landscape and the people (family and friends). Jack can no longer participate the way he used to as far as biking and kayaking and boogie boarding. He cannot play cards or Scrabble or Cornhole. But, instead of focusing on what he cannot do, we need to focus on what he can do. He can walk, watch, and experience. While Anna rides the waves, we take Jack to collect rocks. While Anna goes on a kayaking tour, we take Jack on a nature hike (although with a new double kayak, we are going to take Jack kayaking this weekend). While we play Scrabble, Jack clutches onto Dan or me and is very much part of the game.

It's important that we include Jack in every part of our world. He may not be able to do everything he used to, but he still enjoys the view AND it's our job to provide him with a magical view.

So—GREETINGS FROM BLOCK ISLAND!! We are having a great time. Ray (PopPop) and Sue (Nanna Shoe) are always the most gracious hosts and Mymom and Nonno even came out for a few days. Two weeks in paradise. A perfect end to a great summer.

Enjoy the last week of Summer!

Love, Jess

Those words, written in 2008, seem to capture the attitude that our family took a few more years to fully adopt. I seemed to have a moment on that bicycle where I could really appreciate Jack and his life. While Jack can't do everything, he is part of our experience and seems to enjoy the view.

I'm glad I had this window of perspective just a year post transplant. Most of my memories of these early days are not as positive. I remember being constantly reminded of just how limited Jack's life was and, as a result of his limitations, how limited all of our experiences would be. I spent a great deal of time waiting for improvement and being constantly disappointed by the lack of progress.

Block Island has always been our family's place to relax and recharge. And, it is perfect for Jack. On Block Island, we live without schedules and most of our activities Jack can easily participate in—hiking, beaching, eating. But, like in all parts of our lives, there are always reminders of what ALD stole from our family.

Jack and Anna are the oldest of nine cousins on the Torrey side. They were always the role models of where the others would be in one, two, five years. The expectation was that Jack and Anna would continue their role as pioneers for the cousins. They would be the "firsts"—first steps, first peddles, middle school, high school — maybe even the first to sneak a beer while the adults barbequed on the back deck.

When Jack got sick, he was demoted from oldest cousin to "special" cousin. It was a bit of an adjustment, but most of the crew has grown accustomed to Jack's new role. They know that we need to stay close to the pavilion when we go to the beach, just in case Jack needs a diaper change. They know that they can't let him wander too much in the living room or he will end up finding his way into PopPop and Nanna Sue's room and get stuck. They know that if he is watching TV, they can't change the channel without asking his permission. Jack may be silent, but he is entitled to an opinion and he does prefer Modern Family to SpongeBob.

Not everything came completely naturally to everyone. Jack has managed to lock himself in PopPop and Nanna Sue's room so many times that we all know how to unlatch the door. And, even the adults have been guilty of the channel changing. It's hard to remember to ask our quiet boy when you know the Yankees are on a streak or someone announces that there is a fun movie on. I try to restrain from scolding. After all, Jack seems happy enough having a little company and is not too particular about his TV viewing.

Some of the cousins are extra sympathetic to Jack. His cousin James is always making sure that Jack's favorite channel is on the TV and he is part of whatever activity is going on in the house, "Jack—wanna come be my partner in Scrabble?" or "Let's turn off the TV, Jack. I hear the guys out back playing football."

James is not just sweet to Jack—he is curious. At least once a summer, James will find the opportunity to sit down with me and ask me questions. When he was little, the questions were simple: "How much longer until Jack will speak again?" Now that James is older and his appreciation for the complicated nature of Jack's situation has matured, he presses, "Have you looked into any other treatments that might help Jack?"

Even when I'm caught off guard, I'm always happy to know that James is interested and cares about his oldest cousin, and so I allow him to exhaust his questions for the year. Jack has taught James — taught everyone — so much about compassion without him ever saying a word.

Each year our routine gets easier on Block Island. We know which hikes are easiest for Jack to maneuver and how to get Jack safely into the kayak (that took a while, but it was well worth the effort). We even found an adaptive bike for him to use with Dan. I can't imagine a Torrey August without Block Island. It's our last piece of summer before the bustle of the school year and return to our usual routine.

September 4, 2008

Day +464

Today was the first day of school for both Jack and Anna. We started the day heading down the street to the Annual "First Day of School Breakfast" at our neighbor's house. Last year I remember that as I watched the kids start walking to Jefferson, I started to cry. It was tough knowing that Jack would never walk to Jefferson—perhaps never even return to mainstream school.

What a difference a year makes.

The tang of sadness was there for what could (or should) have been, but today it was overpowered with a sense of relief and excitement. Jack may not be heading to Jefferson this year, but he is heading to school. He has started his new life and he is happy and proud. As the kids lined the steps for the annual photo, Jack sat front and center.

Anna, too, was proud as she got to join the group heading to the upper elementary, Jefferson, as she starts the third grade. Dan, Jack and I walked her to school and kissed her good-luck, though she was eager to join her buddies and start her new adventures. After dropping off our little Banana, I drove Jack for his first day back at school. I wasn't sure how he would react to returning to P.G. Chambers School, but I knew as soon as I pulled into the driveway that he was excited. He gets this look like his eyes are going to pop right out of his head when he is excited and happy.

I managed to get him out of his car seat—a challenge because he was rocking so much—and walked him into school. He was greeted with a dozen staff members all cheering "Hello, Jack!" (It's funny that he knows people that I don't.) Anyway, he did not look back for me when I dropped him at his classroom. He was way too excited to spend the day with his pals. Jack and Anna both share their love for their friends!

Good day all around. I hope all of you moms and dads enjoyed the first day back as much as I did!!

Love, Jess

I was so proud that day that I was able to be strong and acknowledge how far we had come over the last year. I did not shed a tear at the morning breakfast and easily kissed my delighted daughter goodbye at her new school and then my boy at his.

In fact, that day marks the time that Anna surpassed Jack. She was moving on to a school Jack would never attend. She was starting a grade that he would never enter and she would be learning things that he would never be taught. Although Anna is 22 months younger than Jack, she is in many ways his older sibling. It's been eight years since that breakfast and Anna is now 16. She is often asked by us to keep an eye on her brother as Dan and I get stuff done around the house, and she is even sometimes left in charge if we go out locally. We would never leave her with the responsibility of medicating or diapering her older brother, but she clearly has many more responsibilities than her peers.

As a sibling of a person with special needs, she fills a very unique role. Her personality is similar to an only child—confident, strong, and mature. This is largely because she is the only verbal child in our home and she has a lot to say. Our dinner conversations generally revolve around her interests and discussions of her schoolwork/sports/friends. We do, of course, discuss Jack and all his wonderful adventures, but Anna is like a third parent during those discussions.

"What is Jack wearing?" Anna often asks me in an accusatory tone. She's not really asking what he is wearing; she is scolding me because he is not wearing the "right" thing. Anna is a one of those kids in high school—even as an underclassman—with complete confidence. Not only is she an incredible student, but she's an athlete and a person never lacking for people to sit at her lunch table. She knows what is in style for the girls and the boys and she wants her brother to look just as cool as she does. I've tried to get away with the cheaper versions of teen fashion, but Anna always scolds me. "Just 'cause he can't talk doesn't mean he doesn't want the new Nike sneakers."

This confidence transcends every part of Anna's life. When Jack first got sick, we were worried about how Anna would handle her classmates and their questions about her brother. We tried giving her the tools she needed by providing her with honest and appropriate answers to even the most difficult question. "Yes, my brother has been sick, but he's feeling much stronger now." And "Yes, my brother has special needs," and "No, Jack is not able to speak, but he does understand what you're saying."

Although our attempt at holding Anna's hand through the maze of a judgmental world may have helped, I think it's her poise that has helped more than anything. Some of my proudest moments as a mother have been when I've witnessed her defend her brother.

A few years ago, I was snooping on Anna's Instagram (YES—as a mother, I snoop. I need to monitor her correspondence and delete any fishy-lipped photos that sneak through Anna's iPhone). I noticed that she posted a beautiful picture of her and Jack in front of Trinity College in Dublin, Ireland. I smiled to myself, thinking how wonderful that she was showing off both her brother and our trip. The photo gathered 123 likes—unbelievable, knowing I only have 12 followers myself. I glanced down and the comments. "Beautiful," "Jack looks so handsome," "Sweet, Sweet," "Who is the dude? He looks retarded."

I hesitated and read it again: "Who's the dude? He looks retarded."

I told myself that this was why I needed to monitor Anna's social media. My poor daughter must be devastated by this comment. I started to get off the couch to go up and talk to her and suddenly there was a ding alerting me to another comment on Instagram: "That's my brother, Jack. He's handsome and wonderful. His life is a little complicated, but I can promise you that YOU will never be half the person he is."

The dings kept coming quickly as the screen of my phone lit up again and again. People were ripping into this boy that had used the dreaded "R" word in describing Jack. I almost felt sorry for him as I waited to see how the drama would play out.

Finally, the boy responded, "Anna. I had no idea. I'm so sorry."

Seeing the outcome that I had hoped for, I walked up the steep steps to Anna's room on the third floor. I pictured her lying on her bed with tears in her eyes and her iPhone in her hand. I was prepared with hugs and encouragement. Instead, I found her sitting at her desk with her math textbook open and her calculator firmly in her hand. Her iPhone was lying across the room on her bed as if she hadn't given it a second thought.

"Baby. I saw what was happening on Instagram and I thought you might want to talk about it."

Without even glancing up from her book she answered, "What? That stupid comment from Tom? No biggie—he didn't know about Jack. Besides, boys can be jerks about a lot of things. Anyway, I took care of it. I bet he won't make a mistake like that again."

I approached her, trying to figure out if there was a way to share her desk chair, but settled on plopping down on her bed. I tried my best to sound as cool as my teenage daughter, but my voice couldn't help but show my emotion. "You handled it really well."

The crack in my words ripped her eyes from the book. "Please tell me you're not crying. Honestly, Mom, you take this stuff too seriously. You think I've never heard the word 'retarded'?"

"It's just that I'm proud of the way you handled it. I hate that you need to defend your brother and deal with assholes." With that, I sat up and started to walk over to Anna. I didn't care anymore if she needed me—I needed her.

"Mom. It's Jack—you know I'd do anything for him." She could see that her mama needed some attention. She put her book down and allowed me to envelop her with a little love.

Anna was born strong and sweet, but I know that Jack's situation has sharpened these qualities. She, like all of us—even Tom—is a better person because of Jack.

September 26, 2008
Day +486

"Hey Torrey family, this is Tom McCarthey's mom. Please don't apologize for our conversation yesterday. I find it encouraging that you can be stressed about home projects. It means your life has some normalcy to it and not every single breath you take is full of terror about the future. It gave me a strange amount of comfort as another ALD mom."

Perspective. I've been completely stressed out about our kitchen project. I was on the phone last week with another ALD mom and found myself sharing my anxiety about the stove being backordered and the quilted stainless backsplash taking 5-8 weeks for delivery. After venting for a solid twenty minutes, I suddenly caught myself. It seemed ridiculous talking to this mom, who is going through the hell we went through last spring, and sharing something as unimportant as a kitchen makeover.

I have made it my mission to get Jack's story out to the ALD world. I was so tired of reading only the sad stories and felt the need to share our story. I know that Jack has many challenges, and that he is not what is usually considered a success story, but for ALD, he is a miracle. Over the last few weeks, I have been contacted by three different families who are facing their worst nightmare. Each has recently received the diagnosis of ALD. They are learning what they can about the disease and trying to find as much information as possible to help their sons. I have tried to take time each day to respond to these families and be as honest and informative. And, I have tried to give them all some hope.

I try to separate my "hospital mom" hat from "my new life" hat. It means I some-times correspond with a mom in despair and, within the same hour, worry about something as silly as a stove. Yesterday I guess I was wearing both hats at the same time. Again, Mary—I'm so sorry for boring you with ridiculous kitchen stuff and I hope that one day soon, you can stress about something silly like a stove!!

Love, Jess

One year after bringing Jack home from the hospital, I got the brilliant idea that it was time to redo the kitchen. We had planned on the project when we moved into the house two years earlier and had money set aside. I thought I could remind Dan of our plan and sound like I'd reached a place where these types of undertakings were manageable. I could look strong, but he would have the good sense to postpone the project until life got a bit "easier." Instead, Dan said, "Great. Who should we call to do the work?"

I hesitated, waiting for him to take back his words, but he just looked at me with a friendly smile. I tried to sound strong as I said, "Um, I guess I could call around and see who everyone is using these days. You sure this is a good idea?"

"Why not, Jess? Haven't you wanted a new kitchen for a while?"

Of course, he was right. I loved to cook and always dreamed of being able to afford a kitchen with enough burners for cooking Thanksgiving dinner. And there was the island that I'd always pictured my children and their friends clustering around as I doled out their festive snacks. It wasn't a perfect time to dig into something like this, but maybe there was never a perfect time. Besides, didn't we deserve a distraction?

I found the pile of *Kitchens and Baths* and *House Beautiful* magazines that I had stuffed in a closet along with so many unfinished projects. I then started making phone calls. It did feel liberating to be tracking down architects and contractors instead of doctors and therapists. It was also fun to look at all the fancy materials and fixtures. It wasn't until the day that the contractors arrived to demolish the kitchen that it became real.

A cute, muscular guy in his twenties poked his head into the den and said, "Where do you want the fridge? In the living room?"

I suddenly got a knot in my stomach. Our fridge was going to live in our living room? We were going to eat off paper plates? We were going to live without a first floor bathroom? How long was this going to last? What does "four to six months" really mean? Jack was spending most of his time either at school or sitting on the couch in the den. Suddenly we were going to be surrounded with sawdust and hammering. But we had already signed contracts and put down deposits. There was no backing out.

The first couple of days were an adjustment and we did have our moments of "when the hell is this going to end?" but overall it was a fun distraction. As Mary (the ALD mom from the post) said, there was something comforting about the fact that we were moving on with our lives. There was also something almost therapeutic about redoing an old, broken kitchen and making it new and shiny. The parallel was not lost on me.

The contractors became part of our family for those "four to six months"—it was every part of six months in the end. At first they would walk into my command center (the den) if they had a question and try their hardest not to acknowledge Jack—in diapers, sitting on a quilted waterproof pee matt on our very stained leather couch. They never questioned why Jack couldn't speak or walk up the stairs without a great deal of help.

It took a few weeks, but we finally won them over with hot coffee and donuts. Like the nurses on the transplant floor, the workmen appreciated being spoiled and they finally realized that under all the medicine and diapers, we were just a normal, friendly family. They made an effort to give Jack a high-five every morning and gave me a little extra time if I needed to handle a dirty diaper or administer medication during a layout meeting. We became almost family for those months as we worked on rebuilding our family and they worked on rebuilding our kitchen.

One of them had a pregnant wife at home and I tried to calm his nerves that ALD was not a likely outcome for his unborn child. I've since needed to calm the nerves of expecting parents many times. Whether it's talking to parents with typical children or other ALD parents, I have always found sharing our story therapeutic. Finding the right words to guide someone through the trenches of parenthood (with or without illness), helps me better understand what works and what doesn't. It also makes me feel like I have a little control. If not over ALD, at least over my life.

I speak with other ALD mothers often. Many find me on social media or through other ALD families. I think I've become the ALD mom to call if you want a calm voice and optimistic slant on the potential outcome for our boys. I also have the reputation of being a little "lighter" than some of the doom and gloom moms on the websites. I've learned from Jack that a sense of humor goes a long way.

November 14, 2008

Day +534

I have mentioned in past postings that Jack and I have some of our best "con-versations" while waiting for the bus in the morning. We have missed this rou-tine lately. Initially because of being on vacation, and then arriving home to no front stairs to sit on. Yesterday morning we woke up to the sounds of workmen finishing the stairs and announcing that we were safe to walk on them (truth-fully they have not really been safe for quite some time—Dan and I used to call them "the lawsuit waiting to happen"). Jack and I were thrilled to return to our usual routine. We ate quickly, packed his backpack, and sat down on our new front stairs.

I spend much of our time "talking," telling him how proud of him I am and how I love him more than the world. I also spend a little time having him tell me how much he loves me and what a great mom I am (there needs to be some advan-tages to having a son who doesn't talk on his own). This morning, while telling him just how much he loves me, he gave me a look. Kinda like he had eaten a hot pepper. Surprised, shocked, and excited. His eyebrows shot up and his eyes opened extra wide.

I said, "Is that how you are going to tell me that you love me?" and he shrieked and did it again. Perfect. I said, "Jack, do you love me?" and he did his funny face again. It's been a while since he has been able to say the words and I was thrilled to feel the love.

Of course, as soon as Jack got off the bus later that day, I helped him up our new stairs and said, "Jack, I love you" while holding my eyebrows up and opening my eyes like a bug. He giggled and did the same. Who needs to hear the words...

Love, Jess

Like all families, sometimes ours forgets to slow down. Sure, we make time for family meals and often take long walks in the reservation, but sometimes we forget to just sit, enjoy each other, and allow time to simply pass. Waiting on the steps for the bus is a great opportunity to relax without the pressures of modern life. I do sometimes grab the clippers to give Jack a quick manicure. And sometimes can't help but grab the phone to check an email, but generally this time on our brick steps is just Jack and I being together.

Our steps sit in front of our coal-colored center hall colonial, ending in a simple blue stone path to the sidewalk. At 8:00 a.m. our street is buzzing with kids heading off to school and commuters rushing for the train. Jack and I get a handful of waves and good-mornings, but mostly it's just us.

It takes a few minutes to sit Jack down. He has trouble bending on demand. The ALD is ever present when we try to get Jack's body to cooperate. Usually on the second or third try, he manages to bend his knees and settle his bottom onto the top step. I sit down next to him and, without missing a beat, he throws his arm around my neck (it's funny the movements ALD can't steal). Jack's love is strong and I often need to loosen his grip so I don't fall over. And, I always have to remind him not to lick. "Don't lick. Come on Jack—don't do it. No one likes the licking." Part of it is sensory—he tends to mouth things to appreciate where/what they are, but also it's his way of kissing and

I usually give in after some scolding. All the don'ts in the world won't stop him anyway.

We sit and I ask him about his plans for the day and I answer for him according to what I've been told in his school notebook. On Fridays, we talk about our plans for the weekend. And, sometimes, I talk to Jack about my secrets. His big brown eyes are always listening and he is always able to provide me comfort.

If Jack is ever able to speak again, we will be thrilled, but part of me will be a bit worried that he will share some of the things he has heard over the years. I know it's not just my secrets he's heard. Jack has collected stories from anyone who has spent time with him over the last seven years. He will be able to blackmail dozens of people if he gets his words back.

There's something about this time with Jack, my silent child, that reminds me of when I used to nurse my children late at night. I wasn't a dutiful mom when the kids were babies. I didn't adore the little outfits and found reading *The Hungry Caterpillar* day after day a bit boring, but I did love nursing. There was something powerful about being the only person that could feed my children — that they needed me. I didn't even resent the late night feedings, when the rest of the house fell silent except for a baby and me. I did a whole lot of bonding with my kids then. I would talk to them about my dreams for them and sometimes I would share a bit about my own life.

My mornings on the steps with Jack provide me with that same feeling of connection and the appreciation that I am still needed. Jack has a way of crawling inside you, getting so close I lose sight of where he ends and I begin. We become one. We have our morning conversations (only me talking, but he is very much part of the conversation). When the bus pulls up and I walk him up to its doors, I feel relaxed and at peace. It's my morning meditation.

December 1, 2008
Day +551

For those of you who think that I handle things with grace and strength—all that was thrown out of the window this morning. After a good night's sleep (I think that may have been part of the problem — my body isn't used to so much rest), I woke up ready to face the day. I knew that Jack would not go to school because he'd been sick yesterday, but I'd checked in on him during the night and felt confident that he was feeling better. I pictured us watching movies and eating soup until his babysitter arrived and I could escape for a few hours. Even when she called in sick, I didn't worry. It was not a problem. I would put that money right into the Christmas fund and enjoy the day with my boy.

I went into Jack's room at 9:00 and he woke up with his brilliant smile. I felt his head and he was cool as a cucumber . . . good news! Once we were both bathed, dressed, and fed, I sat down to make the dreaded phone call. I knew I had to call the clinic and I knew that there was a possibility that they would make us come in for a check up. I crossed my fingers and hoped they would trust that he was on the mend and allow us to avoid the trip.

Sure enough, after reminding me that Jack's health is still vulnerable (I hardly need to be reminded!!), they insisted on us coming in for more IV antibiotics and blood work. I got off the phone and suddenly I lost it. I screamed and cried and called Dan and cried some more. "When the HELL are we going to get our lives back!! When am I going to have one of those quiet weeks that I've been promised?!?" Trust me, there was no grace or strength and there was way too much focus on how inconvenient this was for me.

We went to the clinic and got to spend six hours of travel and wait time for a 45-minute infusion of antibiotics. I spent most of the time sulking and being rude to everyone around us. Jack even got to watch me as I gave dirty looks to a small, bald girl who was playing with a really loud Tickle Me Elmo (It was driving me CRAZY).

Finally, we got the okay to leave. On our way out, we stopped by the bathroom to change Jack's "grown-up underpants." I was nearly in tears as I wrestled with him to get him changed. I couldn't figure out what was wrong and why I could not get his pants up. It was a further reminder of how complicated our lives have become. Suddenly, Jack started laughing and I looked down. I had put both of his legs into one pant leg. Jack thought it was hysterical. I told him he looked like a mermaid and this got us both laughing so hard that the rest of the day seemed to fade away. Once again, it was Jack who came to the rescue!

Don't get me wrong—I am still in a bad mood. A friend brought us dinner and Dan is being husband of the year, but I think I may need another good night's sleep before I really get out of my funk.

Love, Jess

P.S. Jack is feeling fine and I promise to stop focusing on me...

When you are in the middle of a crisis, you're completely focused on the crisis. Every moment is devoted to the mission. In our case, it was saving Jack's life. It's when you start to remove yourself from the situation that it becomes complicated. It's when you try to balance a normal life with the crisis that you start to resent it. I guess it's actually a sign that you're getting past it. I appreciate that now, but eight years ago, I thought I was going to lose my mind, and I nearly did. In my post, I only shared part of the story of that day.

Jack had been doing great for a while. His health was stable and we were all enjoying our new schedule. Jack had school five days a week. Anna had a mother who could carpool again and be a class mom. Dan had a wife who kept the house organized and managed a smile most nights when he walked in the door. And, I started to have a life no longer controlled by doctor's appointments and diaper changing. I was working on my photography and enjoying the rhythm of our new normal.

I had been startled one day when Jack woke up with a fever, but did not question dropping our new routine to take him to the clinic to be seen. The doctors and nurses did their magic and by the time we left, Jack was feeling better and my heart had stopped racing. By the next day, I'd hoped that we could return to our new normal. I knew that school was not a great idea, but a nice, slow day would be a good compromise. When I called the clinic to share the news that Jack was feeling better, I resented their insistence that we needed to return to see the doctors. "But I have this under control. Jack's fine today and if there are any changes I will bring him in — promise."

The nurse wouldn't budge. "Sorry Jess. The doctor really wants to see him. You know Jack is still vulnerable. We just can't take any chances."

A mixture of anger, frustration and fear bubbled through me as I continued to beg her to allow me to monitor Jack's progress at home. The hospital is only a fifty-minute drive from our house, but nothing is simple or quick when you have a sick child. There is the bag you need to pack, because you are never really certain of the length of your stay. This bag is full of clothes, snacks, medication, G-tube supplies, diapers/wipes, reading material for the long waits and chargers for all of the electronic equipment you can fit in the bag. Then you arrive at the hospital and need to wait for the valet and then find a wheelchair for your son because, although he can walk, you can't manage getting him through the maze of the hospital AND lug the giant bag that you've packed.

I continued to plead with the nurse, but my voice started to fade with my acceptance that nothing would change our new plan for the day. I hung up the phone feeling defeated and began storming around the house, throwing things into the bag and yelling one four-letter word after another. Jack sat perched on his sofa, wearing only a sweatshirt and a diaper. He seemed entertained by his mom's very animated show.

As we got into the car forty minutes later, I was fuming, wondering how long this would last. This life that totally trumped EVERYTHING else. How many more times would we need to drop everything to pack a bag and go to the ER or the clinic? How much longer could I manage this?

What I neglected to mention in my blog was the real truth. That I wasn't just frustrated, I was desperate. As we drove down the highway, not needing to pay much attention to the road that had become second nature, I started wondering if any of this was worth it. Would this new life ever be worth living? Were all of Jack's limitations too much to enjoy any bit of life? Would Jack ever be comfortable again? Would I, as a mother, ever adapt? And what about Anna and Dan? Perhaps their lives would be easier if it just ended. Of course, they would miss us if we were gone, but after the mourning, they could continue on with normal lives.

New Jersey is full of overpasses. High bridges over other highways, creating a web of concrete. These bridges are barely protected by thin, steel guardrails. I wondered how easy it would be to break through the barrier. How quickly would we fall? How quickly would it be over?

I wasn't crying or screaming or out of control. It was the calmest I had felt in a year. A warmth came over me as I saw that I had the power. For the first time in a long time, I could make a choice. This realization was what I needed to keep the steering wheel straight. Knowing that this life was our choice somehow made it bearable. It allowed me to just keep driving toward the hospital.

It had been only a moment, a flash, but it changed my perspective. Not just for that day, but for our future. Nature had taken so much from us, but it didn't take everything. WE had the power to move forward or not, and we were going to choose the former.

When I sat down at the computer that night to write a post, I wrote two. One was my truth and one was for the public. My truth I buried in a folder with other private documents. I couldn't share it with our family and friends, worrying about my complete honesty tarnishing our family's glow. If people knew the thoughts that filled my brain that day, they would know I wasn't just lacking grace, I was a disaster. They wouldn't/ couldn't understand that those thoughts actually made me stronger.

So, I kept the public version pretty. I didn't make up the story about the bald girl with the Tickle Me Elmo or the "mermaid event" in the bathroom, but I did share these anecdotes to distract our readers (maybe even myself) from my ugly thoughts. I always tried to make everyone feel comfortable with our reality. I worried too much honesty would send people running.

Now when I cross that bridge, it's on our way to doctors appointments or emergency rooms, but I still remember the spot where I hit my bottom and realized our power. With this newfound power, life seemed to slip a little further into something I remembered from "Before."

December 24, 2008

Day +572

I wanted to fill you in on many of the wonderful accomplishments Jack has been making. He continues to eat his pasta with gusto and has added pulling candy off our Gingerbread House and popping it effortlessly into his mouth into his repertoire. He has also been eating assorted Christmas ornaments found on the tree...okay, so we aren't quite 100%.

Jack also continues to love school and I think that he has won over everyone at P.G. Chambers School. Today I went to school for his holiday party and, as always, I was amazed at how warm and friendly EVERYONE was to our boy. I am always overwhelmed by the amount of people who take me aside to tell me how magical Jack's smile is. It is amazing how a silent child can speak to so many people.

So Jack is eating, using his hands, laughing and smiling. He's also using the potty (sometimes) and walking up and down the stairs nearly unassisted. All these things are sure signs that Jack is getting stronger and healthier every day. 2008 was (all and all) a good year. 2009 is going to be incredible!!

Merry Christmas, Happy Hanukkah, and Happy New Year!!

Love, Jess

Holidays are always a time for reflection. A time to look back at the year and see where we've come. As I sit and read the words written eight years ago, I'm amazed that life hasn't changed very much. I assumed these small steps would lead to great strides, but it fact, the description here is a fairly accurate description of where we are now. Although everyone who knows Jack agrees that he has made headway over the last eight years, the reality is that Jack in 2008 looks a lot like Jack in 2016.

Today, Jack is still able to eat and eats well. His diet is broad and much more diverse than before he got sick. Jack had been one of those kids who stuck to a narrow, mostly white carbohydrate diet. Pasta and bread were the staples of every meal and the limited protein and vegetables he ingested were disguised in a sauce or stuck onto a slice of pizza. I'd always sworn I wouldn't be one of those mothers who catered to poor eating habits, but when Jack was young and Anna was a baby, I would do anything to avoid a fight with my toddler.

For months following Jack's transplant, he didn't eat anything. All of his nutrition was delivered through a tube in his stomach in the form of formula. We feared he would never eat again, so I fell into my old habits trying to tempt him. Breakfast, lunch, and dinner he would be presented a crispy waffle, a peanut butter and jelly sandwich on white bread (cut in triangles, NOT squares), or a plate of pasta. For over a year the food ended up in the garbage, along with our hopes of his ever eating again. Then, one day he took a few bites. It wasn't immediate, but slowly we realized that every few meals he would eat a bit. It took months, but by December of 2008, we were able to taper down the amount of formula in his tube and rely more fully on his ability to eat.

Drinking is still difficult for Jack. It's actually more challenging to swallow liquid for people with a brain injury than to swallow solid food. It's something about the connection between chewing and swallowing—the information the body is receiving from the act of chewing. For this reason (and perhaps some killing of taste buds during the transplant), texture is now more a priority for Jack than flavor. He loves to crunch, so lettuce and carrots can be as gratifying for him, as can potato chips.

He can even feed himself, but only with a great deal of assistance. Carrots or quesadillas cut into triangles and placed in his hand are a perfect food for our boy. Occasionally, if we put a fork in his hand he will bring it to his mouth, but it's not reliable and a meal would end up taking hours if we left it completely up to him. Also, like Jack in 2008, his limitations seem to disappear when there is a sweet treat around. For a cookie, Jack seems able to do anything. He can reach across a table, even open a bag. He is also still known for eating the uneatable. Oddly, he doesn't ever swallow things that he shouldn't eat, but it doesn't stop him from licking, biting, and munching on such things as crayons, pencils, pennies, and the occasional Christmas ornament.

The toilet training progress has also frozen. Yes, we as caregivers are better trained, and the number of diapers Jack goes through on a given day has shrunk, but he is still far from being as potty trained as a three-year-old. There are just too many parts to using the bathroom. Recognizing when he needs to go is challenging with his particular variety of brain damage. Even if he was able to feel the need, he is far from being prepared to find his way to the bathroom or open the door if he was faced with turning a knob. Jack also cannot unbutton and lower his pants or even sit down on a toilet without a great deal of help. Generally, Jack can't handle activities that require more than a step or two. Using the facilities is something a toddler can handle, but it is simply out of Jack's reach.

While it's difficult realizing his limited progress, I do feel that he is maturing and growing into a young man. His taste in activities is very age appropriate for an eighteen-year-old boy. He wants to see the movies full of speed and action. He wants to be around teenagers and is most happy when surrounded by pretty girls. At school, Jack is still famous for his smile and charm. I often walk unannounced into a classroom for a visit and find Jack surrounded by people. The group is alive with conversation. You would never suspect that in the center of the cluster of people is a boy who hasn't spoken a word in almost ten years.

A happy teenage boy without limitations and control can sometimes lead to the need for apologies on his behalf. Licking strangers, grabbing other people's groceries, walking into displays—a trip to the grocery store with Jack can take over an hour and include many such apologies. Usually a simple explanation and Jack's handsome smile are enough for instant forgiveness. There are, however, some times when he touches a nerve and I'm forced to scold him. It's rare, but it does happen. It took a while following Jack's transplant to finally feel comfortable enough to hold him accountable for his actions, but by the end of 2008, I finally felt safe enough to scold.

December 30, 2008
Day +579

I realized today, as I was yelling at Jack, that I haven't been mad at him for almost 600 days. I think it's proof that we've reached a new stage in our journey.

While clearing out Jack's mouth during lunch (we often need to empty his mouth if he has trouble chewing), he bit me. It was painful and he would not let go. I said, "Come on, Buddy. Stop!"

He bit down harder. "Jack, you're hurting me! That hurts!"

He bit down even harder and only released my finger when he was laughing so hard that he couldn't hold on any more. Jack is 65 pounds and getting stronger every day. My finger was hurt and he was LAUGHING!!

I stood up, pointed my finger at him and told him that he was being mean and it was not nice to hurt his mommy. He kept laughing and laughing. I walked out of the room and did my "count to ten until you calm down" trick. While I was counting, I realized that it has been a really long time since I've been mad at our little guy. Since I felt safe enough to be mad at him. The thought wiped away my anger and put a huge smile on my face.

Dan and I spent so much time being mad at Jack throughout the Fall of 2006 and early 2007. He was not doing his schoolwork and not cooperating at home.

We thought that he was going through a stage, and decided tough love was the answer. Not that we were beating him, but I am surprised that our neighbors did not call Social Services because of the yelling coming from 26 Clinton Avenue.

Once Jack received his diagnosis, the guilt we felt was immeasurable. Jack wasn't being disrespectful and lazy; he had been suffering the effects of ALD. Once we realized what was going on, we felt that Jack was not responsible for anything but making progress.

Now, as Jack is getting stronger, we are starting to realize that it might be time to start holding him responsible for some things—like not hurting his mom. So the time has come that I can get a little mad at Jack. Not too mad, but a little mad.

Love, Jess

One more day until New Year's Day—cannot wait for 2009!!!

Our family sometimes jokes that Jack has masterminded this entire ALD thing as an orchestrated scheme to get away with bad behavior. Although much of his life is complicated and difficult, it must be incredible to enjoy an existence of being completely cared for, where no one requires much from you other than a good smile and a tight hug. This, of course, is our family's way of making light of Jack's significant challenges and trying our hardest to look at the bright side, but there is a little truth behind our joke.

Although Anna laughs with us, she is also quick to point out that Dan and I should do more to discipline Jack. After all, we hold her responsible for her actions. Anna's life, like many of her peers, includes rules, chores, and curfews. Ten years into this new life, and Anna has accepted that all kid chores are left to her. Jack couldn't manage dog-walking or dish-washing without complete assistance. It's rare, but sometimes she breaks and uses words like "unfair" and she is right.

Not only should she not bear the brunt of all the responsibilities, but also I need to remember that Anna needs me as much as Jack does. Siblings of kids with special needs can easily be forgotten. Normal childhood issues can be put on the back burner when complicated struggles can land their siblings in the hospital or worse. Although one might guess that these siblings of children with special needs would resent or rebel against their role in the family, I've found it's quite the opposite. Like Anna, these kids are a remarkable lot—sharing qualities like independence, strength, compassion, and a wicked sense of humor. I've know some of these siblings to start charities at a young age to help causes that have become so much a part of their family. And, I've known many of these children who have selected careers specific to the challenges they've witnessed (doctors, nurses, therapists, etc.). As strong as Anna is (either because of our family or despite it), when Anna's voice breaks, I know that I need to listen.

Even now, years after Jack's transplant, I am still reminded to listen when Anna needs me. Just yesterday, I was on my way home from picking Jack up at school when Anna called. She could barely get the words out. "Mom, I need to go to the doctor. My throat is on fire!"

I glanced at the clock on the dashboard. At 6:00 p.m. we had only two options: the emergency room or urgent care. Both would mean Jack missing his afternoon hydration, a much needed diaper change, and a reasonable dinnertime. I only hesitated for a moment. "I'll call as soon as we pull in the driveway. Let's get you to the doctor."

As Anna got into the car, she seemed to relax, knowing that we were on our way to soothing her sore throat. As we walked into the waiting room, her focus became less about her and more about her brother. Her major concern was that Jack's jeans would fall down. Jack had been sent home from school in "loaner pants" (a result of a bathroom accident). These pants were a size too big. Our family is used to the stares we get when we're out in public, but Anna was eager to avoid any chance of her older brother mooning everyone in the waiting room. I did my best to register Anna and deal with the copay while holding Jack's belt loop.

When Anna needs me, I know I need to listen. I also know that when Anna complains about her pile of responsibilities next to her older brother's, I can't really argue and sometimes ease up on the need for dog walks and laundry loads. I also try to hide the pile of disposable diapers that fill the kids' bathroom by filling the space with teenage girl paraphernalia. Anna seems to appreciate Dan and me listening to her and thanks us with her beautiful smile. A magical smile is something our children share.

Not all Anna's complaints are completely raw and honest. She has mastered when to use her "sister of disabled boy" card. It's often at the mall when she is begging for a new pair of high-priced jeans. She will blurt out things like, "My life is so complicated." As if the jeans will lessen the complexity of having a family defined by Jack's limitations.

Dan and I do often give in, reminding ourselves that Anna's life is more complicated than her friends. If a few pairs of extra jeans can bring out a smile on her face, why not?

I'm certain that parenting experts would disagree with our spoiling of Anna and I'm guessing they might question some of the other parenting decisions we've made. I often play the role of sister to our girl. I've read in many parent magazines that I should always be the "mother, not the friend," but sometimes Anna needs both from me. She doesn't have a sibling to confide in—or a sibling who can verbally commiserate with her teenage angst. I sometimes find myself filling the role of sibling, sitting cross-legged on her bed on Sunday mornings, asking for all the details from the party the night before, trying to be more friend than parent and not to judge so that she feels comfortable. Sometimes she does let down her armor and shares more than she would want her friends to know. I think she needs that from me. I need it too. In fact, maybe it's for me as much as it is for her. We both crave confidants who understand what our life looks like day to day. I hope I don't end up regretting the relationship Anna and I have created. There are no rulebooks for parenting a sibling of a child with special needs. Or maybe there are, but we are just too busy to find them.

It's when Anna remarks about our inability to scold Jack that I have trouble adapting to her wishes. Although the guilt has faded over the last ten years, it's not fully dissolved. I don't think Dan and I will ever fully rid ourselves of the feeling that we should have done more for Jack when he began to unravel. He'd been our first child and we didn't appreciate how unusual his behavior was becoming and tended to blame him for being a lazy/distracted kid instead of searching for the ugly answer. Of course, we did go to a learning specialist and countless doctors, but we also did our share of yelling at our eight-year-old boy whose brain was on fire.

It took time to become accustomed to Jack's new life and his new limitations. We know that he is not able to use the bathroom on his own or make his bed, but we now know that he can turn off the light if we ask him to hit the switch and we know he can feed himself if he is presented with finger food. We do our best to insist that he do these things and we hold him accountable if he is too aggressive with the dogs or walks into the street without holding securely onto someone's hand. We also finally feel completely comfortable scolding him if he bites anyone. Luckily, it's not a common occurrence.

January 9, 2009

Day +589

Some days I feel like I am living two completely different lives. One is the "Jesse" I have been for years—wife, mommy, daughter, friend. Sometimes a little flaky, but basically a good person. Fun, lighthearted, tends to drink too much wine with her friends, and takes a good photograph. I'm also a "hospital mom." This person is part nurse and understands words like "chimerism" and "demyelination." This person worries about outliving her son—then worries about him outliving her.

Like most people, many times a day I find myself at the computer, checking emails, Facebook, and CaringBridge. Within a sitting, I can find myself writing to one friend about the latest book club selection and another about the loss of vision that their son has recently experienced. Just the other day, I started corresponding with a mother who lost one boy to ALD, is starting the transplant process with her other son, and has a daughter fighting cancer. Just moments later, I corresponded with an old friend who needed a recipe for chicken.

I've been told that it's the way our minds work, allowing us to compartmentalize different facets of our lives. I guess it's what keeps me sane (or perhaps what defines me as nuts). My friends and family who have less complicated lives often apologize for complaining about the little things (misbehaving children, misbehaving husbands, lingering colds). Truthfully, I like nothing better than being part of those conversations. Splinters hurt. Sure, they are not fatal, but they are real. Having one part of my life feel normal is a luxury that I could not live without.

I hope all you other hospital moms get a little bit of normal each day.

Sorry for the rant. I am having one of those mornings that is a little too quiet and with too much time to reflect. I've been looking forward to these slow, quiet, post-holiday days, but I am not so sure they are good for me. I think I am going to go out and take some pictures...or I could start exercising...or, maybe I will finish my book.

Love, Jess

Everyone has different sides to their personality. Mine is just a little more scattered than most. My Facebook feed is a constant reminder of my dueling lives. I've topped out at over 800 friends and it's a broad assortment of people from many chapters of my life. When I was first introduced to Facebook, I tried to separate my lives. I filled it with friends from childhood, college, and graduate school. Facebook was the fun, non-ALD world where I could be silly and share memories. While I didn't hide the reality of my complicated life, it wasn't the focus and it was liberating.

Several months into my Facebook account, I got a friend request from a woman with whom I'd become quite close. She had a son, diagnosed with ALD just days from Jack. She and I would correspond daily, sharing details about our experiences as we each witnessed our sons go through the torture of transplant and then begin their journey into a new life full of challenges and complications.

I felt strange combining my playful Facebook life with hers. Like mixing oil and water, I worried there was no way for my two lives to merge. Part of this was that I was concerned that she (and the rest of my ALD world) would be shocked at hearing about my life, which was not always focused on our limitations. By this point in 2009, Dan and I had worked hard to resurrect a bit of our former life. There were photos and stories all over my Facebook page that I thought might be too fun for my ALD families to see. I worried that seeing this other side of me would make me look as though I wasn't taking our new role as special needs parents seriously enough.

I was also worried about my current Facebook friends seeing the reality of what life looks like with a profoundly disabled child. Few people can truly appreciate what it is like to have a child with disabilities. It's not just the constant care—it's the constant concern for what the future will bring. Our lives prove that bad things do happen to good people and no amount of prayers or Holy Water can fix our broken children. I had been able to share this with my ALD friends, but wasn't sure that I was ready for my other friends to see that side of my life.

As I hit *Confirm,* I knew that I was taking the next step in our new life. I was introducing two factions of our reality and allowing them to sort it out. The result has been quite wonderful. My ALD friends enjoy the fact that our special family does have a rather normal life—despite the diapers, special schools, and doctor appointments. And my other friends have also appreciated that a special family can be quite normal. They've come to know Jack and have learned that complicated lives don't have to be sad, and families can work under the most complex of circumstances.

February 19, 2009

Day +629

When Jack was a couple of months old, I took him to a baby group in Chatham, NJ. For those of you not from NJ, Chatham is a charming suburb of New York— full of beautiful, blond, wealthy people. Walking into the "New Moms" meeting, I instantly felt like my hair was not blond enough, I was not dressed up enough, and the fact that I did not bring a nanny made me a little self-conscious. What made me feel better was that I had the perfect baby. He may not have had on a perfectly matching Ralph Lauren outfit, but his smile was larger than life.

We sat in a circle and listened to everyone share their experiences as first time mothers, and I started to feel a little less self-conscious. I even started to think that I might be able to find some friends there. Then, Jack pooped. Not a little discreet poop, but one of those poops that oozes up the back of the diaper and suddenly moves through the clothing to reach every inch of everything around.

I held Jack up to find that he had also managed to soil me completely. I got up as inconspicuously as possible, and ran to the bathroom. Thankfully, I managed to grab my diaper bag and tried to relax as I told myself that I shouldn't wor- ry, I had another outfit for Jack. Then I realized that I had used the extra outfit the day before after a messy incident at the grocery store. Thirty minutes after escaping to the restroom, I returned to the group with a naked baby in my arms and my own clothing still covered in feces. Needless to say, I said a quick good- bye and ran out the door NEVER to return. That was almost ten years ago.

This morning, I walked into Jack's bedroom to be overwhelmed by the smell of poop. Unfortunately, it isn't a rare occurrence to find that Jack has soiled himself during the night. I held my breath and assessed the situation. Nothing was contained about this bowel movement. A shower was the only solution. I got Jack out of bed and walked him as carefully as possible to the bathroom. Getting his shirt off made matters worse and poop splattered all over the floor. I yelled "Stop moving!!" to Jack and "Stop eating the poop!" to Finn (what is wrong with this dog?). I wrestled Jack into the shower and scrubbed him down.

As I toweled him off, I still smelled poop, but I kept looking and surmised that it must just be lingering in the air. I got Jack dressed, got the laundry started, got Jack's feeds in him, gave him his medication, fed him a waffle (I am not super mom—thank goodness for Eggo), and got him outside to meet the bus. The whole time we were going through our morning routine, Jack and I were laughing and making poop jokes. The bus came, I walked Jack out, wished all the kids a good day, walked inside, and went to the bathroom to wash my hands. As I glanced in the mirror, I realized that I had a large smear of poop on my sleeve.

I thought back to the day at the Chatham "New Moms" meeting and smiled. If only I could go back now. Now, I know how to laugh.

Love, Jess

I've never been afraid of poop. Not that I enjoyed it or discussed it often, but I've always been a bit of a tomboy when it came to such things. Remembering that day at the mothers' group in Chatham brought back memories of feeling so inadequate. I think young mothers often do, no matter how prepared they think they are before delivering their new human. And, for some odd reason, I chose to go to a neighboring town for the mothers' group. As I said in my post, it was a town full of well-moneyed blondes who all seemed to regain their pre-baby bodies in record time and have no problem finding a break from their new babies to grab a manicure and a highlight. I, on the other hand, was sporting broken nails and hair that hadn't seen a beauty salon in months. I was also a relatively young mother in comparison. Most of the group had a solid ten years on me. I could have found this brag-worthy, but instead I found it intimidating. I guessed that their extra time living somehow made them more prepared for motherhood.

As I stood in the bathroom trying to figure out what I was going to do, I wondered what was wrong with me in choosing this group and what was wrong with these women that not one of them thought to check up on this young mother lost in the bathroom for half an hour. Jack's episode actually gave me a wonderful excuse to escape and luckily I did find another mommy group quickly. It was full of other broken-nailed mothers with roots in their hair and daily uniforms of stretchy pants. Many of these women are still dear friends of mine today. They've been part of our journey from the beginning and have provided a great deal of support. They have cried with me and held me up, and they have also laughed with me along the way.

It took a while to find the laughter, but one gift that ALD has given our family is a huge amount of perspective. Things like poop and matching outfits no longer seem important, and scenes like the one we had at the mothers' group in Chatham would put a smile on my face and not tears in my eyes now.

I'm not a believer that "things happen for a reason" and I certainly don't believe in a grand plan that could make sense out of all the horror that we've seen—the horror that Jack has suffered. But, I do think it's important for us to grow through our experiences. Our experiences have certainly provided us with an enormous amount of growth. Growth that has made us stronger and allows us to understand and appreciate what really matters. Once we reached this place, we were able to move forward and start picking up the pieces of our lives.

March 2, 2009
Day +640

We have gotten accustomed to our new life pretty well. We're used to the diapers, the medication, feeding Jack by hand, and hydrating him through a tube.
Even the not talking. Jack is happy and in a great school. We're able to travel
again and sometimes days go by without the mention of ALD.

The thing that we will never get used to is watching Jack sit on the sidelines. He
observes more than participates. I don't think Jack minds too much, but for Dan
and me, it is depressing to see him watching others do things that he once was
able to do. On Saturday, Jack got the opportunity to get off the sidelines and be
a doer.

The students at P.G. Chambers School were invited to participate in a winter
sports event hosted by The Best Day Foundation (www.bestdayfoundation.
org). We drove up to Thunder Ridge Ski Resort and were greeted by a group
of incredible volunteers working together to make a great day for 15 "special"
children. As we were signing in, Jack was assigned two volunteers to help him
through the day. They were two of the cutest teenage girls and Jack would have
been happy just to sit with his two new friends and look at them. They took us
around and Jack got to check out the petting zoo, a winter obstacle course, and
go tubing. He loved the tubing. His new girlfriends helped Jack climb to the top
of a hill, sat him on a tube and sent him flying down the hill. It was incredible to
watch him get to experience the adventure. Jack is a lucky boy!

Love, Jess

March 5, 2009
Day +643

Yesterday was a big first for Jack and me. We changed his G-tube for the first time. It's the tube that goes directly into Jack's stomach and needs to be removed and replaced every couple of months. It's not a complicated procedure, but I've always waited for his doctors to do it for me. This month, I decided it was time I learn how to do it myself. It's imperative that I learn how to completely care for our boy. It's not quite as much fun as some of the other firsts Jack and I have had, but it was a milestone I will always remember. I feel oddly empowered!!

I am heading out of town today for a weekend with my girlfriends. It's the fifth year I have managed to steal away with some of my pals to enjoy time in the sun. We eat, drink, sleep, and chat. We also play cards, dice, and solve the problems of the world. One year, I remember talking non-stop about how Jack was driving me nuts and the next year, I talked about celebrating his first year post-transplant. Without my girlfriends, I do not know how I would survive.

Getting out of the house for three days is a challenge. I have my lists and numbers and back-up plans. I have Mymom coming out and a sitter helping and Dan as leader of the team. If you see my family this weekend, be nice!!

Love, Jess

Mar 23, 2009
Day +661

Yesterday was one of my proudest moments as a parent. A painting of Jack's was selected to be included in a touring exhibit for Very Special Arts (VSA). We were invited to the VSA Meet the Artists Reception. Jack had the largest entourage of any of the artists. Twelve in all, we walked around the show and quickly found Jack's painting, "My Beautiful Hands." We were all amazed.

Jack's art teacher had been trying for months to find a way for Jack to express himself artistically. Making art had been one of Jack's favorite things, but his new challenges made creating difficult for him. She tried different techniques and finally found something that worked. Using a special brush, she only had to hold his elbow to initiate his arm. Jack was able to select each color and create his painting. It's the most beautiful painting I've ever seen.

Love, Jess

May 27, 2009
Day +728

Our application is officially complete with Canine Companions for Independence (CCI)!! There are still a few more steps before we introduce a new member to our family, but we are happy to be moving forward with the process. Many people have asked how Jack would benefit from a service/companion dog. Our number one answer is friendship.

Friends have always been very important for Dan and me, and I think we've passed that on to our children. One of the saddest parts about Jack's new life is that he's not been able to maintain many of his friendships. It's not that his buddies are mean and don't care about him, it's that Jack can't keep up with them. He can't walk to town for ice cream, or play video games or capture the flag. He tends to watch and sometimes he gets a little lost. I don't think it bothers him too much, but for Dan and me it's depressing. Luckily, he has his "love" cousins and "blood" cousins, who never forget to include him in their fun and games—thanks guys. And, of course, Jack has Anna and his school friends too, but wouldn't it be great for Jack to have a four-legged friend to keep him company?

A few weeks ago when we were in Baltimore to see Jack's ALD specialist, we met a little boy with a CCI dog. Although it was difficult for the little boy to look us in the eyes, he introduced his dog to us and allowed us to shake his hand (the dog, not the boy). I asked the father about their experience with CCI. He told us how magical the relationship was between his son and his new best friend. Then, he got a little teary and said, "Now my son is not just the boy with autism. He's the boy with a really cool dog."

Love, Jess

We were finally settling into our new life. There was no magic day that we realized we had arrived at our new normal, just an appreciation that time had gone by without constant fear and lengthy discussions surrounding doctors, medications, or therapies. Of course, many days still included mentions of doctors and medications, but those words no longer hit our core. And we started to figure out how we were going to make the best of this new life.

Years earlier, if you had told me that I would be able to give my child IV medication and change his diapers and G-tubes, I would have balked. I was a nice person and a good mother, but not the kind of individual who embraced change easily, or ever volunteered for the extreme. Jack's illness did not ask politely for commitment—it demanded it. So, I learned how to care for him. I put my fears aside, took a deep breath, and dove in. In doing so, I realized that nothing I was doing was without a support system. Our doctors were always available and we had friends and family willing to help at a moment's notice. And we, our family, were a stronger team then we ever imagined. I may have been the primary caregiver, but Dan has always been a close second, often coming home from a long day at the office to roll up his sleeves and give Jack a shower or draw some medication. And Anna, even as a young girl, has never hesitated to help when needed. We also have been lucky to afford and find a small army of wonderful people to help us when we need a break. Learning to let others help has been a lifesaver for us. Not only does it give us time to rebuild our strength, but it reminds us that we are not alone and not indispensable. It's far less pressure to know you are not the only one who can care for your child. So many things were necessary to keep our family strong.

This strength came from all the people who held us up, and we really flourished when we accepted our new reality and stopped resenting it. We were able to appreciate just how different our lives were, but that different didn't mean that we had to sit back and just let the disease (and Jack's challenges) rule our lives. Participating in events like The Best Day Foundation and Very Special Arts were our first introductions to a surprisingly broad world of interesting programs for people with disabilities. When I speak with other parents of special needs children, I always encourage them to check out what's available in their local communities. It's not just for the child; it's for the whole family. There is something so normal when you're able to see your child participating. Their experiences might look a little different than those of their peers, but when you see the smile on their faces, their challenges seem to disappear.

Of course, even participating in adaptive programs doesn't completely dissolve the reality that life is complicated, and we were always looking for things that would help make Jack feel better. When a friend mentioned the idea of a service dog, we discussed the pros and cons of adding a new member to our family. It didn't take long before we were filling out our application and waiting anxiously on the waiting list. Keegan has now been part of our family for almost five years. Technically, he is Jack's skilled companion, but truthfully, he is our family's companion. All of us share a special relationship with our four-legged friend.

It wasn't just Jack who needed to participate in the normal. We all needed to be reminded to start living again. Anna was only six when our lives changed and has the luxury of not remembering life before. She simply lives her life knowing that her reality is a bit more complicated than many of her peers', but that she has a family that supports her in all her endeavors. It seems to me to be working out for her when I see her smile, flawless grades, and domination on the lacrosse field. Dan and I also managed to learn to thrive in our new reality. We promised ourselves that we would not to allow our limitations to prevent us from enjoying life. Like Jack's adventures, ours sometimes need to be a little adapted because of situation, but we don't let it stop us.

May 15, 2009
Day +716

Question: When Jack was sick, would you have donated blood on his behalf? Would you have donated platelets? Would you have been tested to be a bone marrow donor for him? Would you have donated your child's umbilical cord blood?

Two years ago, we didn't have the luxury of time to ask you. Like seventy percent of people who need a stem cell transplant, Jack did not have a match within the family and we needed to rely on donors. And Jack didn't just have a stem cell transplant—he had dozens of transfusions while he was in the hospital. For weeks, he needed blood and platelets every day. Jack's life was literally saved by strangers. We've often focused on "The Little Lady from Detroit" who provided Jack with those crucial stem cells, but I don't think we've focused enough on the other heroes who helped save Jack.

In honor of Jack's birthdays (his two year old transplant birthday and his eleven year old traditional birthday), we are thinking of throwing a Drive/Party. What do you all think? Would you come to 26 Clinton Avenue and swab your gums to join the bone marrow registry? Would you give a pint of blood? Would it help if you could look at Jack's smile while you became a hero?

26 Clinton Avenue has been known for quite a few parties, but I think this could be the biggest yet!!

I am really asking for everyone's input. Without your help, this can't happen.

Love, Jess

July 25, 2009
Day +785

Today is the big day—**Jack's Bone Marrow Birthday Party!!** Jack woke up with a huge smile on his face and danced around the upstairs when we reminded him that today was the big day! We weren't able to get the Red Cross truck to come for blood donations, but we are ready to sign up people for the Bone Marrow Registry. Donations saved Jack's life and we hope that someday someone from today's party will have the luxury of giving someone the gift of hope.

If you haven't officially RSVP'd, it's not too late—come, enjoy Jack's magical smile, swab your cheeks, and have a cupcake.

Love, Jess

Jul 27, 2009
Day +787

200 cupcakes + 125 people celebrating Jack + 79 new people joining the registry + raising over $2300 = a house full of proud and exhausted Torreys!!

This weekend's Bone Marrow Birthday Party was amazing! To see the house and yard filled with people who have helped and supported us for the last two years was incredible. And to have so many people register was inspiring. Jack's smile lit up the party from start to finish. Thank you all for joining us. Even those of you who could not be there were there in spirit. Thank you, thank you, thank you!!!

Love, Jess

The party was extraordinary. It was a beautiful summer day and we ended up filling our home with over a hundred people. We had burgers grilling on the BBQ, cupcakes galore, and cold drinks filling coolers. Kids played basketball in the driveway and drew elaborate murals with sidewalk chalk in front of our house as their parents swabbed their cheeks to join the National Bone Marrow Registry. I had help from another ALD mother who organizes drives all over the country in memory of her son who had lost his battle with our ugly disease. She sent me a huge box with registration kits and trained me to set up the drive. I was a little hesitant to be trusted managing a drive along with a party, but I did it. With a team of eager, organized friends, we registered 79 people that day.

As proud as I am of our accomplishment, a bone marrow drive is not nearly as complicated as I had anticipated. There are no stretchers, IVs, or need for medical staff. There is simply some paperwork to fill out and cotton swabs to catch the DNA from the inside of the cheek. The whole process takes about 15 minutes.

The most complicated part of hosting a drive is educating people and taking the fear out of a procedure that conjures up images of long needles and lots of pain. For a girl who nearly failed ninth grade biology, by the time we hosted that party, I had learned quite a bit about the procedure that saved my son's life.

The first statistic that I shared with the folks who came to the drive was that 70 percent of people who need a transplant do not have a match within their family and there are approximately 12,000 people that are looking for a donor at any given time. Having them add their information to the list is the first step to giving a person (a family) hope. One in 40 registered members will be called for initial testing. One in 500 will actually donate.

Then, I would dive into the information that people are panicked about—the actual donation. The donation process is not nearly as frightening as one would think. There are three ways to donate stem cells—bone marrow donation, peripheral blood stem cell (PBSC) donation, and through umbilical cord blood. Traditional bone marrow donation is a surgical procedure where doctors withdraw liquid marrow from the back of the pelvic bone. Donors receive anesthesia and feel no pain during the procedure and the recovery is as quick as a couple of days. PBSC donation is a non-surgical procedure where the patient is injected with a drug, which promotes an increase of the number of blood-forming cells in the bloodstream. After five days, blood is removed through a needle in one arm, passes through a machine to extract the needed cells, and then the blood is returned through the other arm. I've known people who have donated this way and returned to work the following day. The last method is how Jack's stem cells were donated—umbilical cord blood. After a healthy birth, the baby's umbilical cord can be privately stored or donated to a public bank (otherwise those precious cells are literally thrown away as medical waste). There is absolutely no pain or inconvenience to the baby or the mother.

We didn't need to do much arm twisting and registered 79 people at the party. Three of our friends who registered that day have gotten the initial call, and one donated their bone marrow last year. A life was literally saved from something as easy as a BBQ. Since that day, we have hosted quite a few drives and know of four people who have donated after being inspired by Jack to join the registry.

When Jack first got sick, our family spent a great deal of time asking WHY??? Why did this happen to Jack—to our family? Why does he need to suffer? Why can't Anna have a typical brother? Why did Jack lose his speech, his independence? These questions are understandable, but ultimately are questions that have no answers. As the years have moved forward, our goal became to direct our energy toward a different list of questions. Questions that provide us with power. Questions that start with the word HOW. How can we move forward and enjoy our lives through the challenges? How can we help others going through similar situations? How can we pay it forward? Hosting bone marrow drives, hosting parties, raising awareness — these are the answers that give us power.

Jul 7, 2009
Day +769

We're home from our Block Island 4th of July Adventure! Great time had by all, but especially Jack. He got to go to the beach, watch the parade (no Torrey float this year), watch the fireworks, play with his cousins, and eat and eat and eat. With eight kiddies running around PopPop and Nanna Sue's house, it's amazing how much you appreciate one silent child...I'm kidding (we adore all our nieces and nephews).

I do think that sometimes Dan and I forget that Jack doesn't speak. It's just part of our new normal. Besides, Jack seems to speak fairly well with just his eyes. I do love hearing the chatter of all the other children racing around the house. I sit pretending not to listen as they talk about things. Kids can be so silly, but they can also be quite wise. I had a few really interesting conversations about Jack with the under-five bracket.

At the local grocery store on Block Island, I was busy shopping and let go of Jack's hand. I saw him out of the corner of my eye as he slowly approached a little boy with his big (almost creepy) smile. The little boy looked up at Jack and said "Hi." Jack just kept on smiling and stepped so close to the boy that I was worried he might squash him. I quickly grabbed Jack's hand and apologized to the boy and his mother. "Sorry. That's how my son says hello."

The boy just looked at me and said, "Wouldn't it just be easier if he talked?"

I paused only a second, "Well, yes. It sure would be easier, but he can't talk."

His eyes then focused on Jack as he processed what I had said. His mother seemed a little uncomfortable, but I assured her with a smile that it was okay. The boy looked back at me and said, "Can you tell him that I hope he has a nice day?"

With that, Jack smiled and gave the boy a high five. "Looks like he heard you. He wants you to have a good day, too."

On July 4th, my niece Anne approached me and told me that "Jack is really quiet now, but my mom says that once he gets feeling better, he'll talk again."

I explained that I hoped that her mother was right and started to explain the scientific reason for Jack's loss of speech and the variety of therapies we were trying to help retrieve his words. She looked bored and interrupted, "Aunt Jesse, I know he's going to talk again because my mother said so."

With that, she grabbed her buggy board and headed down to the water. Life is so simple when you are young.

We are so lucky to have our Torrey family reunion every year on Block Island. Our family is incredible and for an island that's only three miles by seven miles, it is jammed packed with beauty and magic.

Love, Jess

Oct 16, 2009
Day +870

Dan and I are home from an amazing trip to Paris. We were non-stop tourists, trying to seep in every ounce of the city. The art, the churches, the food, the wine, the cafes—we took in all we could. I know I should say that Dan and I had a difficult time separating from the kids, but we were so busy that we spent very little time focusing on them. Besides, we felt completely confident that they were in good hands. And they were.

We arrived home to the house not only still standing, but with homemade bread and a cake on the kitchen island, happy kids, and groceries in the fridge. Anna and Jack seemed to have a great time and I think my parents enjoyed it, too. They even mentioned "the next time you and Dan get away"...

Waking up this morning was wonderful. I got to make myself a cafe au lait (thanks to Mymom's milk foamer) and woke up the kiddies with a newfound appreciation for everything. In fact, when Jack peed on me in the bathroom, my first reaction was not to use a four-letter word. Instead I smiled and congratulated him for getting so close to la toilette.

Love, Jess

Travel is something that drew Dan and me to each other early in our relationship. Dan speaks several languages and studied in Paraguay and Italy. He grew up with a father who, as an airline pilot, taught his children to travel fearlessly. I grew up with our second home being in Chile and parents who preferred European holidays to beach vacations. Dan and I both enjoyed exploring museums and churches and also loved our weeks away that only required packing a bathing suit and shorts.

When we first got married, Dan and I dreamed of one day being transferred abroad. Being able to share our love of travel with our children. When the reality of Jack's life became apparent, we realized that we no longer had the ability to uproot our family for an extended period, but we still wanted to travel.

Block Island was our first adventure—just a year after Jack's transplant. My in-laws live their full time and checked with the local medical center that, in case of emergency, they had the ability to care for their oldest grandson. They also set up our room with any comfort they thought might make our stay easier, and I packed more medicine than Jack would realistically need for a year. Ironically, we found out a few weeks before we left that one of Jack's doctors was vacationing on the island the very same week. It made the removed little island feel much closer to home. Sometimes our family is lucky.

Block Island is perhaps the easiest place for our family to vacation. In fact, it might be the easiest place for our family to be. Not only do we have family there, but Block Island is also on "Jack Speed." Real life is full and fast. We have a big house and big lives and constant activity. It's often impossible for Jack to keep up. The result is that Jack spends much of his life watching—either us or the TV. On Block Island, our lives are at Jack's pace.

We stay in a tiny two-bedroom cottage on my in-laws property. A bit removed from the commotion of the festivities, it allows us to join in on the fun and escape when needed. Days on Block Island are slow and activity is all Jack-friendly. Our biggest accomplishments each day are a bike ride, finishing a puzzle, making chowder, or going to the beach. Our biggest responsibilities are grabbing groceries and throwing in some laundry. Jack gets to enjoy everything and the rest of us get to slow down. Everyone should try to spend more time on "Jack Speed"—trust me, the world would be a better place ;-)

We never miss our big family reunion every Fourth of July and now we also enjoy the month of August each summer with sand between our toes on Block Island, where the only worry is running out of sunscreen. It's just what our family needs to recharge before the commotion of returning to school.

Our family has also managed to venture farther and farther as the years have gone by. I was so nervous as Dan and I planned our trip to Paris, but my parents insisted, going so far as to book our airline tickets so that we wouldn't back out. Once we landed at Charles De Gaulle Airport, our worries vanished. And when we arrived home six days later and realized how well it had gone for the kids, we were thrilled. It was liberating to know that we could get away for not just a night out, but several days. Since then, we've made an effort to get away (just the two of us) at least once a year.

We've also gotten rather adventurous as a family. The Make-a-Wish Foundation sent us on an incredible vacation in 2010 and it taught us that plane travel wasn't impossible. The following year, we went to Florida again. Our confidence led us to plan a trip to Ireland. Then, two years later, to Italy. Traveling with a special needs child is intimidating, but we are lucky that Jack is very comfortable and content, even when off schedule. We know to call the airline ahead of time to request a wheelchair for the airport. Although Jack can manage the walk through the lines, it is much easier to have him safely in a chair. We also know to travel with an assortment of notes from doctors answering any questions people might have about his medical requirements. Luckily, we've never needed a foreign hospital, but I think we would manage.

Whether we are touring a museum or enjoying a view, Jack keeps up with us every step of the way. He loves sightseeing, big meals, and the warm smiles that he gets out of strangers. Our biggest concerns usually center around toileting, but we have found that travel is worth learning to change a diaper at 35,000 feet.

Feb 24, 2010
Day +1001

From Dan (AKA Daddy)

What have you done during the past 1,000 days? What has happened in your life during that span of time? Are you a different person today? Or has the time passed seemingly without notice? Is your world a different place?

Today marks 1,000 days since my son, Jack, received a stem cell transplant to save his life. In the most basic terms, he has lived for the past 1,000 days. And for that fact, our family is grateful beyond words. He has been forced to learn how to live a new life—a different life than he had before Adrenoleukodystrophy interrupted his old one. He has learned how to live again and we have learned with him.

Jack has learned how to walk again and how to eat again. He never forgot how to smile or how to laugh. He has learned what it means to have a healthy appetite. And his appetite for life never wanes. He takes none of it for granted.

So much has changed on this planet in the past 1,000 days.... America elected its first African-American President. Wall Street crashed. Bear Stearns, Lehman Bros, and Merrill Lynch ceased to exist. GM is now run by the Federal Government. Eliot Spitzer got busted. The Yankees won another World Series. The Giants — and even the Saints! — won Super Bowls. Hurricanes, earthquakes, global warming, 22 inches of snow in Baltimore...Jack Bauer still hasn't gone to sleep yet. Kings of Leon released three more albums before they decided to sell out for good. We discovered the Snuggie.

Our extended family has had much to celebrate. Weddings...graduations...the birth of many new cousins—too many to count. Life goes on, we all get older, and we try to embrace the changes.

And Jack has done so many, many wonderful things in the past 1,000 days. He has entered a new school that he loves. He rides the bus every day with his classmates. He has made tons of new friends there and elsewhere. Jack has gone hiking with his dad. He has played with his dog. He has watched his sister grow up. He swam as much as possible (he always loved the water). He has helped MyMom in the kitchen. He has watched countless hours of awful reality TV with his Mom and sister — and loved every minute of it. More drama!

And then there were the adventures...he rode roller coasters at Disney World, got the VIP treatment all over the park, swam with dolphins at Discovery Cove, received an once-in-a-lifetime tour of Yankee Stadium, and met the players and coaches — even Derek Jeter! He flirted with cheerleaders at the Jets game. There were trips to Block Island — swimming, kayaking, sailing (and puking), clamming, playing with his crazy cousins...He went surfing at the Jersey Shore and snow tubing and sledding in the Catskills. He even hunted Jackalopes. He laughed and laughed with his friends until he wet himself, and then he laughed some more.

But there are many things that Jack could not do during the past 1,000 days. He did not speak a sentence — only a stray word here or there. He did not ride his bike or his scooter. He still has trouble getting down the stairs by himself. He stopped singing — we'll never know why. He did not learn about NJ history in social studies class, nor long division in math. He did not move on to 3rd grade...

or 4th grade...or 5th grade. Jack may never get to do any of these things. But he will make the most of what he has in this new life. Just yesterday—on Day T + 999—he wrote his name in class.

Jack endured so much pain and trauma during the first 100 days. But all of that has been reduced to distant memory, followed by 900 days of progress, happiness, discovery, peace, joy... LIFE. Today, we celebrate an anniversary of a life that we do not take for granted.

Here's to next 10,000 days...20,000 days...30,000 days...of Jack's life.

Love, Dan

Dan's words captured every bit of where we were and where we'd been at Day +1000. 1000 days and we were in many ways a new family, and our core was as solid as ever. We had been through hell, but we had managed to stay on track with our goal of happiness.

It wasn't one event that changed our perspective. Life is rarely that simple. It took time and patience and a great amount of support. It took the constant fear of more complications to fade. And it also took a magical boy who has a way of making things better with something as simple as a smile.

I'd be lying if I said that I wake up every morning optimistic and loving every aspect of this new life. I'd be lying if I said I didn't sometimes lie in bed, in the safety of the dark, crying for my son, for my family, for the life I thought we would all have. I watch our friends as they prepare their kids for college (kids that used to play with Jack on the playground as children). I congratulate their accomplishments as I clench my fists and remind myself to breathe—and to smile. It's no one's fault that Jack can't join them. Anna has quickly grown and surpassed Jack to become his big sister (although she is two years younger). She is the sibling who protects and looks out for her brother. She adores him, but she is also becoming more and more independent and will soon leave home for her own adventures. Children are supposed to leave. I sometimes daydream about what Dan and I would ever do if we had an empty nest, and then I cringe knowing the only way our nest will ever empty.

We don't have a clear prognosis for Jack. There are only a few boys who have shared his particular form of ALD and course of treatment. Some of those boys are doing well and some have not done so well. There seems to be no specific reason for the outcome. Not knowing Jack's future could have us in knots, but instead we choose to focus on the positive. He is happy now and, with the exception of the brain damage, epilepsy, and Addison's disease, he is healthy and strong (I don't say those words easily, but honestly). Although Jack's life is more fragile than most, none of us really know when our time will be up. We all have the responsibility to live our lives appreciating every day. Appreciating every day and every moment is how Jack lives his life.

I'm not religious enough to feel confident that this life is just the beginning of an eternity, that this is just a small chapter and that we will have the luxury of easier days to look forward to. If this is the only life we have, I don't want to waste it with the what-ifs. I have a responsibility to my children to be a role model. I'm not always great with eating veggies or avoiding four letter words, but I can show my children how to appreciate life and what we do have and not dwell too much on what we're missing.

We have an intact family and a loving extended family, always willing to help. We have piles of friends who are there to celebrate the good times and rally during the hard times. We have the financial resources to pay for added help and support and fun (I'm very aware that not all families in our situation are as comfortable financially). And, perhaps the key to our family's success, we have a child who lives in the moment and is happy today.

I often say that I will not allow ALD to define our family, but that isn't really true. It is a huge part of our family. But, even with ALD, we are still the Torreys—happy even though this all happened. Let's face it; no one is blessed with a life without complications. Our complications are more pronounced than most, but if you ever met us, I think you would agree that we are doing really well. It's taken a lot—family, friends, neighbors, doctors, nurses, teachers. It's like we're held together with duct tape. Not pretty, but super strong.

Epilogue

Day +2001

Last night we had dinner with friends. It's one of the few things that hasn't changed in our new life. Our friends still love to find any excuse to entertain. A beautiful summer Sunday, burgers on the grill, kids running around the lawn. It was lovely.

As always, Jack sat perched between two worlds, sitting on the deck with the grown-ups while the other children played in the yard, overhearing inappropriate adult conversations as his peers played tag and kickball. Periodically, one of the adults would bring him down so that he could "be one of the kids," but he always found his way back onto the deck. He doesn't mind being a spectator.

After dinner, one of our friends' daughters tapped me on the back to get my attention.

"Mrs. Torrey, why is Jack so quiet?"

That used to be a hard question to answer, but now I have my response at the ready. "Well, Lily, remember when Jack got sick a few years ago? He lost a lot of things and one of them was his words."

"You mean he can't talk?"

"That's right. He can't talk right now, but I bet someday he'll be able to again."

"Is anyone helping him?"

"Oh yes. We have an army of people that are helping him."

"That's good. I sure hope he gets his words back." She seemed satisfied and started to walk away. I smiled to myself. I've had this conversation countless times and it seems to be getting easier. Most kids just need a simple explanation to satisfy them. They're much easier than adults. Then, Lily turned around and asked the most incredible question.

"Mrs. Torrey, can Jack laugh?"

"Oh yes! Jack loves to laugh. Come here and let's make him laugh together."

We sat at the table and easily made Jack do what he does best. Whether Jack ever talks again is a mystery, but until then, we will enjoy every minute of his laughter. His laughter is what gets us through each day of our not so new life.

Love, Jess

About the Author

Jesse Torrey's life ticked all the boxes. She had a degree in Fine Arts from Goucher College and a Master's in Art Education from New York University. She was married to a wonderful man, had two perfect children, and enjoyed careers as an art teacher and a photographer. But in 2007, her life and family suddenly fell apart. Her son Jack was diagnosed with a rare disease that left him with more health issues than she ever thought possible. Initially, Jesse started writing to keep her friends and family aware of Jack's progress. Now, ten years later, she's come to accept her family's new normal and writes to share her never-ending mission to create a ordinary life with a special child on her blog, www.smilesandducttape.com. Some days are more successful than others, but she continues to find peace and laughter even in the most unexpected circumstances.

Jesse lives in Maplewood, New Jersey with her husband, Dan, her children, Jack and Anna, and their dogs, Keegan and Finn.

CPSIA information can be obtained
at www.ICGtesting.com
Printed in the USA
BVOW08s0224071116
467109BV00001B/111/P